Quarterly Essay

Quarterly Essay is published four times a year by Black Inc., an imprint of Schwartz Books Pty Ltd. Publisher: Morry Schwartz.

ISBN 9781760642761 ISSN 1832-0953

Subscriptions – 1 year print & digital (4 issues): $79.95 within Australia incl. GST. Outside Australia $119.95. 2 years print & digital (8 issues): $149.95 within Australia incl. GST. 1 year digital only: $49.95.

Payment may be made by Mastercard or Visa, or by cheque made out to Schwartz Books. Payment includes postage and handling.

To subscribe, fill out and post the subscription card or form inside this issue, or subscribe online:

quarterlyessay.com
subscribe@blackincbooks.com
Phone: 61 3 9486 0288

Correspondence should be addressed to:

The Editor, Quarterly Essay
Level 1, 221 Drummond Street
Carlton VIC 3053 Australia
Phone: 61 3 9486 0288 / Fax: 61 3 9011 6106
Email: quarterlyessay@blackincbooks.com

Editor: Chris Feik. Management: Elisabeth Young. Publicity: Anna Lensky. Design: Guy Mirabella. Assistant Editor: Kirstie Innes-Will. Production Coordinator: Marilyn de Castro. Typesetting: Marilyn de Castro.

Printed in Australia by McPherson's Printing Group. The paper used to produce this book comes from wood grown in sustainable forests.

THE END OF CERTAINTY

Scott Morrison and Pandemic Politics

Katharine Murphy

When Scott Morrison and I sit down to talk, it's not yet clear whether the coronavirus is going to jump its containment lines, triggering a significant second wave. Infections have spiked in Victoria, and the trend looks grim, but Australia has flattened the curve before. We are supposed to be good at this.

These are some of the last hours in which Morrison hoped the second wave in Victoria could be avoided. When I realise this later, the insight feels transgressive, as if I've stumbled into somebody's private space, even though this is nonsense – there is nothing private about a man's hope when the country he leads is suspended between two possibilities: successful suppression and a rising body count. In any case, hope will expire shortly after we speak. Victoria's premier, Daniel Andrews, will lock down public housing towers in inner Melbourne, close the border with New South Wales, then he'll lock down the city, and Morrison will stand in his courtyard in Canberra and declare that today we are all Melburnians.

Just before my arrival on a Friday afternoon, Morrison has been on the phone to Andrews. The prime minister and the premier are close. Actually, that's not quite right, at least not in the way the term is commonly understood in human relationships. Perhaps it's truer to say they have each other's measure. Each sees a person he can work with. When it suits their interests, or when frustrations boil over, the opposite is also true: Morrison and Andrews go to war, usually covertly, sometimes overtly, a couple of big cats pacing and prowling the open-range zoo of politics. But Morrison says his relationship with Andrews is "the key fusion" in the federation – the glue that holds Australia's pandemic response together, even though the two leaders have not always agreed. Andrews has been the evangelist for lockdowns and Morrison has cajoled the premiers towards reopening. So it's ironic, given this dynamic, that the first state to battle a second wave was Victoria, because the state government failed in the enforcement of hotel quarantine.

Andrews spent months warning Victorians they were a heartbeat away from catastrophe, a precautionary drumbeat that made him a whipping boy in circles inclined to believe with a force bordering on fervour that commerce must always prevail, that livelihoods trump lives. The virus chose not to make a liar out of the premier just as Australians had begun to hope that the worst would be something we would read about, rather than experience; just as we'd come to invest in the idea of our own exceptionalism. 2020 is a cruel year, a terrible bastard, and the reversal in Victoria as winter began to bite felt wanton enough to exemplify the cruelty.

The age of social distancing requires interviews to be conducted at safe reach. Morrison and I sit at opposite ends of the communal table in his parliament house office. The last time I was in the prime ministerial office, Malcolm Turnbull was at the head of the table serving some kind of health-enhancing tea. This was reasonably early in Turnbull's tenure, before the deputations arrived and the walls closed in. Given the limited shelf-life of Australian prime ministers over the past decade, I've come to think of this office as a private Gethsemane, a place where the trickle of vanquished men, and Julia Gillard, endured their five stages of grief, then summoned the resolve to make the final journey to the stone courtyard just outside to have their crucifixions narrated live by David Speers in his Sky News days.

The current custodian of the space would understand my whimsy, but I'm sure sees his lair quite differently. Shortly after the election, one of Morrison's senior advisers told me on the sidelines of an event that the posse was settling in for a long stay. "We'll be here a while," he reported, in the placid tone of a man who thinks he's cracked a code. That's what they all think, of course, and perhaps this crew will evade the anguished indignity of defenestration, or the terrible indifference of the people. But during my professional lifetime, longevity has been a quirk of a bygone era. Only John Howard has managed it.

Last time around, I was listening to Turnbull narrate his prime ministership while surreptitiously eyeing off a handsome John Olsen on the wall. This time, out of the corner of my right eye, I think I see a small grinning garden gnome on a shelf. Morrison looks tired, but I've seen him grey-washed over the past few months, in his press briefing room late at night, willing himself not to sway on his feet.

I'm amazed this conversation is happening at all. The interview, long promised but elusive, has been put back by fifteen minutes, then thirty, then an hour, polite little bleeps in my WhatsApp, because events are crowding in. Victoria is in trouble, and the government in Canberra is meeting around the clock to determine what to do with the income support rolled out during the crisis. The Indigenous affairs minister, Ken Wyatt, is also wearing out the carpet in the corridor as he perambulates slowly, but with purpose, between the ministerial wing and the lift to the committee rooms, something otherworldly in his gait. There's a meeting of peak Indigenous groups underway upstairs.

Morrison is fully extended. There's not a lot of bandwidth for sharing, or delving, and I suspect very limited tolerance for it. All prime ministers are interviewed on high rotation. It's part of the job. But Morrison's outings are almost exclusively in the "yes mate" genre. Talkback. Paul Murray on Sky News at night. 2GB with the new Alan Jones. Sometimes Ray Hadley, but not much, not since he asked Morrison to swear on a Bible, an affront killing a fine bromance stone-dead. Neil Mitchell in Melbourne when he has to. That creaking baritone whose name I can't remember on Adelaide commercial radio. Sometimes, *A Current Affair*. Political alphas develop a method to keep intimacy and insight at bay: relentless patter punctuated with bursts of micro-aggression. The prime minister treats his "yes mate" outings like open mic nights. Heckling, if you encounter it, and mostly you don't, is immaterial, as long you land the line.

Mining and interpreting the line is the stock-in-trade of the Canberra press gallery journalist. We chase the daily increments with the relentlessness of cats chasing flickering lights or small prey. But I'm not here for a new line. I'm trying to bear witness. I want to document what it has been like to be prime minister at this moment. I want to record and analyse these extraordinary times, and understand how Morrison is shaping them, because if I understand that, I'll capture a prime minister in flight, at a critical moment.

But Morrison's objective right now isn't to be understood. He'll tolerate this conversation, he might even enjoy bits of it if we both choose to be present and avoid lapsing into passive aggression, but being understood is not really his purpose. He's a perpetual-motion machine, a man of verbs. I suspect reflections happen, but safely outside this theatre, because musing in politics is akin to napping. It makes you vulnerable.

His opening gambit as we take our seats is "I haven't done a lot of this." He means sit-down conversations during the pandemic, or indeed at all during his prime ministership. There's an implication in the unsolicited situation report: he's not certain this interview should be happening. I'm not a media intimate of the prime minister. I don't know the secret handshake of the "yes mate" club. Morrison and I bump along convivially enough, but periodically I irritate him, and we both know I'm not of much use to him. So don't expect much sharing. I turn on the recorder and pick up my pen.

As we settle into the back and forth, we both agree that it is hard to keep the basic facts and events of COVID-19 straight; it feels like years have passed. At one point in the conversation, he prefaces an observation with "what I said to the party room many years ago when I became leader." For the record, that was less than two years ago, but he's right, 2020 has been a decade, and we are only at the midpoint. I tell him it took me about three days to construct an accurate timeline for this essay. Morrison says his memory is terrible. "I have a flow brain," he says. I've never heard of a flow brain. When I look it up later, I discover it is a cognitive state associated with peak mental performance. Apparently, flow brain means you are in the zone, when your skill level is equal to the challenge before you.

We work through questions and answers until we reach the nub of what I want to ask. The pandemic is at a pivot point, and the government is neck-deep in deliberations about how to navigate this tremendously challenging period, a period Morrison has, correctly in my view, compared to the two most dangerous decades of the twentieth century. Morrison says one of the problems with the deliberations is that you are required to make decisions with imperfect information. Officials give you material. A lot of it is helpful. But it doesn't tell you what to do. He says he makes the upper echelons of the government drill concepts into submission, describing his deliberative method as "things come up and up and up, you shave them off, you smash them out, you bring other people in." What he means is that proposals go around the room many times until there is a satisfactory resolution. If there's not enough certainty in the room, then other perspectives are sought. He thinks the extent of the drilling might frustrate his colleagues. After half a second's thought, he adjusts that to "exhaust" rather than frustrate.

"Are the hardest decisions in front of you, or behind you?"

"It's a good question," Morrison says. There's a pause while the prime minister mulls.

Watching him gather his thoughts, I'm curious. Will the response be a formulation, or an answer? I leave the silence there, and in the silence, Morrison chooses truth.

"I hope they are behind us, but I'm not convinced," he says. "That's my honest answer."

It's hard to know where to begin with this event, because it is profound enough to have unmoored humanity. We are off-balance. We want to stop worrying about the virus, but we know we can't, because the crisis isn't over and we don't know when it will be. Before the pandemic, we'd grown blasé about convenience. If something ached, you took a pill. If you wanted food at 10 p.m., a gig economy worker brought it to you. Now, inconvenience asserts itself in daily life. There are limits to our agency. We are vulnerable. While some of us have been underwhelmed by the risks, seeing the virus as a beat-up or someone else's problem, many of us have weighed the most mundane of tasks, attaching risk assessments to routine activity. Our ingenuity hasn't yet produced an effective treatment, or a cure, leaving us impatient, restless and anxious. We remember what life was like before the pandemic, when we hugged everyone with reckless abandon and didn't wash our hands, but we don't know what is ahead of us.

Pre-COVID, Australians were fleet-footed citizens of the world, roaming far and wide, and now we need a permit to cross state borders. Friends in Melbourne say the second lockdown, with its night-time curfew and Defence doorknockers, felt more oppressive than the first, like an arbitrary punishment – although polls suggest the community is firmly behind the measures. New South Wales is on tenterhooks. As a journalist chronicling the long days of the most significant global crisis since the Great Depression, I find readers increasingly fretful. Some want you to question everything and everyone. Others want the questions to stop to preserve equanimity in the herd. *Lay off, will you, everyone is doing their best.* Questions are signposts to failure, and we don't want our leaders to fail, because if they fail, we are the casualties. Australians will tolerate mistakes, so long as the effort succeeds.

Given this pandemic is disorientation, given that's the new normal, it seems sensible to start our story at the beginning. Let's roll back to January

2020 and capture the months that saw Australia dive under the first wave rather than be dumped forcefully on the sand.

Australia's attorney-general, Christian Porter, has two obsessions. The first, politics, you probably could have guessed. That is likely mandatory, given his family background. Porter's grandfather served in the ministry of Joh Bjelke-Petersen and his father was a director of the Liberal Party in Western Australia. Porter studied politics, economics and law at university, before practising law, including as a prosecutor in Western Australia, before entering state parliament, and switching across to federal parliament. Neat, orderly, linear progression. Porter's second obsession is post-apocalyptic science fiction. That's an overhang from childhood. He watched *Mad Max* before he was supposed to, before responsible adults deemed the content suitable. "There is a joke we have in our family. Whenever there's something on the news, someone will say, 'That is how the apocalypse starts,' because I've watched so many sci-fi films where they start with a news grab of some obscure event. I can list you out the films that start that way: *The Edge of Tomorrow* with Tom Cruise – that starts with an obscure piece of news about a comet crashing in the background. There must be 100 films that start that way."

Porter was recharging with his family over the New Year break. "It was after Christmas, early January, when the first reports were coming out in the news about an illness with flu-like symptoms in Wuhan. I said, just jokingly, because we always say this in my family: 'This is how the apocalypse starts.'"

In post-apocalyptic science fiction, audiences, the ardent fans like Porter, are fluent in the conventions. Part of the joy in the genre is the formula. Generally, the obscure news report is followed promptly by concrete evidence of the alien invasion or the zombie apocalypse. Nobody has to wonder for very long whether or not this is a real problem, because the lizard-tongued CGI alien arrives in the town square with the blaster, and the smiting starts. There is nothing to fear from the spectacle. It's not real life. Nothing is actually on the line. The worst it can get is spilling a choc-top down your shirt during a jump scare.

Morrison has already flagged the difficulty of decision-making with imperfect information, but there was a simpler risk in January. It would have been very easy to miss the arrival of COVID-19. Back then, in Australia, citizens and politicians were heavily preoccupied with the most catastrophic bushfire season in more than a century. Reports of a strange virus in China seemed very remote to me in Canberra, as we packed up our baby photos and identity documents and worked through our bushfire survival plan, with the blaze menacing the western edge of the city.

The summer was terrible. Heat had arrived in November, followed by the choking smoke. Late in the month, giant hailstones pelted down in Canberra, shredding foliage, destroying vehicles, smashing in skylights. Australians weren't contemplating a second apocalypse because they were too busy battling the first. People hoped that 2020 had already delivered its worst. *No worst, there is none. Pitched past pitch of grief.*

This goes to one of the challenges of crisis management. Sometimes there is obviously, categorically, an existential threat: wildfires across three states roaring across roads, tearing into towns, snuffing out the summer sun in the middle of the day, fire fronts with sufficient squalling fury to generate their own weather patterns, humans huddling close to the water with whatever they could carry, native birds raining dead from the sky. That's a crisis, a textbook example – although Scott Morrison took far too long to grasp it. The coronavirus was different. It arrived quietly, when our collective anxieties and efforts were trained elsewhere.

Australia's chief medical officer, Brendan Murphy, was in Rome, with his family, in an apartment 200 metres from the Trevi Fountain, entirely unaware they were holidaying at what would shortly become one of the epicentres of a global health disaster. Two months later, the Italian health system would be overwhelmed by people dying from a new virus that authorities had failed to see coming or contain; clinicians would be forced to play God, deciding which patients would get a ventilator. Morrison was mishandling the bushfires in full public view, struggling to find his metier, and then working around the clock to regain control. From the middle of

January, he was also battling the sports rorts controversy that would cost Bridget McKenzie her front-bench spot and drive the Nationals into a frenzy that erupted on the opening day of parliament. The chances of missing this particular crisis were compounded because China was less than transparent about what was happening there. Only severe cases were reported, which understated the threat.

By the time Brendan Murphy was back in Australia, on 12 January, news reports were gathering pace about the novel betacoronavirus known as 2019-nCoV. He returned to work immediately. A cluster of viral pneumonia cases had surfaced in Wuhan, in China's Hubei province, during December. The World Health Organization's China office was informed of the development on 31 December. Chinese state media had reported the first death from the illness as Murphy was flying home from Italy.

In the middle of the third week of January, Murphy was interviewed by ABC Radio in Melbourne. He told the ABC there were fifty cases in the city of Wuhan. Recalling those opening weeks, the chief medical officer says the main problem right at the beginning was lack of concrete information. "We weren't sure whether there was any human-to-human transmission, and there was a claim that there were no more cases in the past week – so it sounded like it was an animal vector with not very good human-to-human transmission."

Soon the opposite was true. "Better information came out of China in the next week and it was very clear there was a significantly growing outbreak and there was human-to-human transmission. I think there were early health worker infections. Suddenly the whole picture changed. A virus that is not efficiently spread from human to human, that comes from [an] animal vector, is very easy to control, but once you've got human-to-human transmission and growing case numbers – that's a whole different ball game."

The whole different ball game triggered Australia's pandemic plan. A report was prepared for the prime minister and the health minister, Greg Hunt, on 21 January. According to that brief, there were 221 cases of

COVID-19. Four deaths had been reported. There were 198 cases in Wuhan, and nineteen in other regions of China. Four cases were known to have been exported: two in Thailand, one in Japan and one in South Korea. In Queensland, health officials were also testing a man with coronavirus symptoms who had returned from Wuhan. Ground zero of the outbreak appeared to be the Huanan Seafood Wholesale Market, although there was speculation among senior Australian officials that the source of the virus might have been a laboratory in Wuhan. (More about the Wuhan lab theory shortly.) In any case, after a health alert was issued by Chinese authorities, the wet market was shuttered on 1 January.

The WHO had issued travel advice on 10 January, but had not yet recommended any travel or trade restrictions. It would not declare a public health emergency until 30 January. Murphy, in his capacity as Director of Human Biosecurity, moved ahead anyway, declaring "human coronavirus with pandemic potential" a listed human disease under section 42 of the *Biosecurity Act*. The listing on 21 January allowed restriction of flights from Wuhan to Australia. The National Incident Room was already operating to help manage the bushfire response; soon, the pandemic gave it a dual purpose. Murphy also spoke to his counterparts in America and the United Kingdom to compare notes. It was still unclear to Australian officials how severe the illness was, and there wasn't clear evidence about the likely incubation period.

Shortly after the Australian advice went to Morrison and Hunt, on 23 January, the Chinese regime locked down Wuhan, as Murphy puts it: "Aggressively, as only the Chinese can do." On 24 January, the respected medical journal *The Lancet* published a study flagging likely human-to-human transmission of the new coronavirus. The study looked at the early COVID-19 hospital patients in Wuhan. It noted the first fatal case, "who had continuous exposure to the market, was admitted to hospital because of a seven-day history of fever, cough, and dyspnoea. Five days after illness onset, his wife, a 53-year-old woman who had no known history of exposure to the market, also presented with pneumonia and was hospitalised in the isolation ward." By 28 January, Queensland had its first confirmed case. The man in his forties was put into isolation at the Gold Coast University Hospital. The day after that, the state government declared a public health emergency. Australia's public health response was about to accelerate. On 1 February, Australia imposed a travel ban on China. US President Donald Trump had signalled his intention to do the same the day before, and the world was clearly moving in that direction.

I asked Morrison when he first comprehended the gravity of the situation. He said the economic consequences of COVID-19 were clear to him reasonably early, certainly by late January. China had suspended tour groups to Australia, a significant source of tourism income, and the government was deliberating about the border ban. "When you have to shut your border to China, you realise you are in for quite a time economically," he says. "Making the call to shut the border ran over three days." The process started on 22 January, the day before Morrison's father, John, died. On the day of his father's death, Morrison went to Tumut, Batlow and Tumbarumba. "We were doing bushfire stuff. When we came back ... I went to the pandemic response centre over at Health and met and spoke with them again. That was the night my Dad passed away, and from there we were very much into understanding the full import of this. We were moving into a completely different phase. The economic side of this for me was very significant right from the start, but it was still unclear at that time what the nature of this virus was from a health point of view."

Imposing the travel ban seems entirely obvious now, but it was a bold move, given the importance of the China relationship to Australia's prosperity. Quite apart from the practicalities of lost income and earnings, the regime in Beijing would not be pleased with Canberra's diplomatic affront. Brendan Murphy tells me that making that call was one of the moments in the crisis when he felt most stressed. The WHO had not recommended travel bans at that time, and China promptly blasted Australia's "overreaction."

Beijing wasn't the only stakeholder reacting furiously. One senior official recalls how all hell broke loose domestically once it became clear what the Australian government intended to do. "It was the weekend before university was going back, school was going back. The vice-chancellors just completely lost it when they realised they weren't going to get their international students back," the official recalls. "It was very hard back then to paint the picture of what was going to happen if we didn't ban travel."

The same official, who spoke to me on a background basis, posits that Australia shut the border quickly because of concern the virus was not a naturally occurring phenomenon, but the possible consequence of a laboratory accident – a leak from the Wuhan Institute of Virology, which had been doing work on bat coronaviruses. The official says that risk – the risk that the virus came from a laboratory, not a wet market, that it might have been more virulent – was discussed right at the beginning among Australia's chief medical officers, the experts who were trying to risk-manage the opening days of a crisis.

The Wuhan lab leak theory simmered away in the background, until it became supercharged when the Trump administration tried to promulgate the conspiracy in order to deflect attention from its own mismanagement of the crisis. The lab story then careened around Rupert Murdoch's media outlets in America and Australia, amplifying the whodunnit. As geopolitical tensions flared, dragging Australia into a boxing match between the two great powers, our two most important partners, the tale became so lurid that it was difficult to sort fact from fiction.

The facts are still hard to fully untangle because of the diplomatic sensitivities, but Murphy says health officials here, right at the beginning, did speculate about the possibility of a lab accident in Wuhan because of the sort of research that was being carried out in the city. But he insists Australia closed the border with China because of "the epidemiology in China – nothing to do with suspicion of a lab accident ... But of course, we speculated. The reason a lot of people speculated about the source of the virus was – it's one of the unusual features of this particular coronavirus compared to, say, SARS or MERS – just how readily it has adapted to infecting humans. Generally, when you jump species, it takes a fair bit of mutating before you can readily adapt to spreading in another species. But that is probably just an accident of nature."

I'm keen to nail this point: was the possibility of a lab accident a risk Australia was actively managing at that time or not? Does this risk management explain why we were quick to shut the borders regardless of the consequences? "Looking at all the evidence, published articles in *The Lancet* and others, it seems pretty likely it was a natural phenomenon," Murphy says. "We certainly had a discussion early on about how this virus had come about – but that discussion had nothing to do with the decision to close the borders."

Scott Morrison recounts the deliberations this way: "There was that speculation at the time, but it never got better than speculation. We had nothing to back that up. The virus was coming out of Wuhan like a freight train. My view was it was always more likely to have come out of the wildlife wet market, and that seems to be the weight of evidence – but there was a virus lab in Wuhan." He says the speculation wasn't "people thinking it had been deliberately let out, the speculation was about misadventure." Morrison says the place of origin was beside the point:

> We knew it was coming out of Wuhan – where it started was less the issue. We just knew it was coming, and it just had to be shut down as fast as possible. What we were more concerned about when we were shutting the borders to China was the levels of protection within China – we were worried a wave would rush across China and we didn't want to be late on that. It turns out China had done a better job of containing it within Wuhan than we were calculating at the time – that said, zero regrets on the decision. Absolutely zero.

Murphy explains why the border closure call was fraught in a public health sense. It offended established international verities about pandemic management. "The public health mantra, and the WHO has always said this ..." – he chuckles – "well, they did, is you don't ever close borders, that's not a helpful thing to do in a pandemic. When we took border measures, some of our colleagues in other countries questioned the value or the merit of doing it. It was out of kilter with conventional wisdom. But we thought this has a higher mortality rate than flu, significantly higher mortality, and [it is] a lot more infectious than SARS and MERS, so it could really take off. We just decided whatever the public health mantra, we're not going to stick with it."

Morrison says the border closure, aided by the "discipline" of Australia's Chinese community in self-isolating after returning home from visits to the mainland before hotel quarantine became mandatory, "prevented that first wave hitting Australia – that was the wave that wiped out Europe."

I'm curious about what happened in America, then, given the devastation there. Trump closed the border with China at the same time. Morrison says he doesn't know why the difference was so marked. "It suggests to me there were already a number of cases there without people knowing. COVID got more of a foothold before their border ban kicked in, and I don't know what procedures they put in place."

Murphy is clear about the elements of Australia's public health strategy that choked off the first wave of infections: border closures, testing, tracing, and enforced quarantine for all returning travellers. That strategy, he says, was the difference between flattening the curve and running behind an uncontrolled outbreak.

Restrictions were imposed on flights from Wuhan as soon as it was clear the illness could be transmitted in the community. Murphy says that he is reasonably confident health authorities traced all the early cases exported to Australia from China and that, critically, Australia also had an established network to expedite testing. The Doherty Institute, a Melbourne-based medical research facility, worked quickly once the virus had been sequenced. "They grew the virus and we got testing up and running, and we deliberately put it into our public health lab networks, which are a well-established network of labs that are part of our health protection system," he says. "We established initially in-house tests before the commercial test kits became available."

Two premiers, Victoria's Daniel Andrews and Queensland's Annastacia Palaszczuk, have claimed credit for insisting that all returning travellers submit to a fourteen-day compulsory hotel quarantine, the issue that would go on to cause Andrews grief. But Murphy corrects the two politicians in a low-key way. He says it was his idea. "I put it to the Australian Health Protection Principal Committee and we took it to the national cabinet." The AHPPC is the rolling committee of Commonwealth, state and territory chief medical officers. "We didn't think they'd go for it, then Daniel Andrews strongly supported it. He led it at the national cabinet ultimately, and Queensland supported it very strongly. When we took it to the national cabinet, we were surprised at the enthusiasm by the premiers."

As well as the border closure, and hotel quarantine, Australia also locked down all non-essential services to help flatten the curve. Professor Jodie McVernon, who is the director of epidemiology at the Doherty Institute and one of the key infectious disease experts advising the Australian government on the spread of COVID-19, offers a useful insight.

McVernon says after the Chinese regime shut down Wuhan, other governments and their public health advisers around the world began to realise that economy-wide lockdowns could form part of managing the pandemic. "There is not a country in the world that in their pandemic plan even mentions lockdown," she says. "It was well beyond anything that we considered conceivable." But after the Chinese authorities locked down Wuhan, and liberal democracies in Europe started following suit, "we realised this was in our toolkit now."

The Australian government possessed sweeping powers under the legislation Murphy deployed on 21 January: the *Biosecurity Act*. Under this framework, government authorities designated by the chief medical officer can make control orders forcing individuals to remain isolated at a medical facility or quarantined in their homes. The health minister also has the power to determine "any requirement that he or she is satisfied is necessary" to prevent the entry or spread of a disease. The emergency powers are draconian, but the legislation passed the parliament in 2015 without any fuss, largely because the proposal was bipartisan. These health provisions sat quietly on the books, unused until coronavirus.

Porter, the attorney-general, said that lack of prior use necessitated a significant scramble in the opening weeks, because the regulatory processes were rolling off the production line for the first time. "All this was done from scratch," he says. When he explained the scope of the existing powers during radio interviews early in the crisis, listeners were astonished, doubtless because this was the first time they had heard about the framework. "People thought I'd lost my mind, that I was a fascist," he chuckles.

McVernon notes another key early event that focused public and political minds on the risk of COVID becoming an uncontrolled pandemic. Researchers at Imperial College London released modelling in mid-March showing that an unmanaged outbreak would overwhelm everyone, not just China. The modellers found that an unmitigated epidemic could see 510,000 deaths in the United Kingdom and 2.2 million in the United States. Those findings ricocheted around the world and triggered an abrupt reversal of the "herd immunity" strategy favoured by the British government. Herd immunity happens when a substantial proportion of the population becomes immune to a virus either because they have recovered after infection or because they have been vaccinated.

In the middle of March, Australia's deputy chief medical officer, Paul Kelly, suggested officials here were looking at potential infection rates of between 20 per cent and 60 per cent of the population, which led to headlines that up to 150,000 Australians could die at the peak. Doherty Institute modelling released three weeks later indicated that an uncontrolled pandemic would see demand for intensive-care beds peak at 35,000 per day.

"The Imperial model was very useful for all of us because it did put out there the uncomfortable truth that an unmitigated epidemic would overwhelm everyone," McVernon says. "We all looked at Wuhan. We all did the maths. We all brought it back to our governments and said, 'This is going to happen.'" McVernon says one of the unpleasant truths in all this was that until infections started to run away in Europe and the United States, "we didn't really believe this applied to us." She says she finds that reality "uncomfortable."

Debate about the utility of the modelling has persisted through the crisis, in Australia and around the world. Questions were raised initially here about whether the modelling led political leaders into locking down more services than was warranted. University of New South Wales epidemiologist Professor Raina MacIntyre says the job of the competent pandemic planner is to identify the worst case and work backwards. "Pandemic planning is preparing for the worst-case scenario and hoping that that's not going to eventuate," she told a Senate committee hearing in June. "The modelling numbers that were discussed at the beginning were the potential worst-case scenario. We did not get that because of the strong actions and disease control measures that were taken in Australia."

Another health expert at the same hearing, the Australian National University's Professor Peter Collignon, begged to differ. "I actually think there are troubles with a lot of the models that were put out. I think Imperial College London was way over with its estimations, and I must say the ones in Australia [are] as well. MacIntyre had a prediction of 10,000 deaths before the end of May. I was reading *The Canberra Times* thinking, 'I can't see why we would do so badly.' I predicted a few hundred deaths by the end of May, and I'm pleased I'm wrong and I overestimated." Collignon said the problem with the models is that they rely on an assumption about the spread of a disease called R_0 (or R nought), "which is the reproduction number if you do nothing about it and if you have a completely non-immune population. That is not real world and will never be real world. I actually think those models that do that are ridiculous, basically." Collingnon's point is that pandemics inevitably trigger interventions, so running a model assuming a do-nothing response adds little or no value.

There is obviously debate between experts about the measures taken:

what worked and what didn't, what we might have done better, whether models were helpful or whether they drove politicians into an economy-destroying panic. Murphy, the expert managing the crisis, has outlined his checklist for success. But he also nominates one more, far simpler factor to explain why things worked initially here, but didn't work elsewhere. Australian politicians acted on the medical advice. They respected scientific evidence.

What Murphy says is not entirely true. Politicians didn't always strictly apply the medical advice; in fact, they often front-ran it. The bulk of the medical advice during the first wave never suggested shutting down schools, for example, "but then," as one official puts it, "you put a teachers' union in the mix, and parents, and Victoria giving nobody any room to move, and you get a different result." Someone familiar with the rolling deliberations of the chief medical officers at the AHPPC says there was never any medical advice to close playgrounds, for example. Closing state borders wasn't recommended during the opening months of the pandemic. But political leaders closed them anyway. Leaders took the expert medical advice as an input, not an absolute. They listened to health advisers, but politics wasn't suspended. The medical advice was processed through a political lens.

But Murphy's point stands in the way he means it: politicians in this country trusted experts. They didn't feel compelled to construct ever more elaborate alternative facts.

During one of my interviews with Murphy, I asked him whether he knew Anthony Fauci, the American physician and immunologist who is the director of the National Institute of Allergy and Infectious Diseases in the United States – the scientist who emerged during the crisis as a low-key foil to the gross negligence of Donald Trump. In rancorously divided America, Fauci became a folk hero for many onlookers when he lifted his palm to his forehead during one of Trump's early unhinged monologues, and he also became a target of the far right. Murphy chuckled at the question. "Not really, no. I've met him once, the poor bugger. We've been talking to people at the Centers for Disease Control and Prevention and they were pretty frustrated early on in the outbreak." Only frustrated? "I'm being diplomatic," Murphy says.

Murphy repeated his assessment: the clear difference between Australia, the UK and the US, if you boil it down, is that Australian governments accepted the medical advice, "and they have acted on it." This is such a modest mission statement, the idea that policy during a pandemic threatening lives and livelihoods would be evidence-based. But the observation hangs uncomfortably between us because of the alternative it evokes. Murphy lives in a world where the expert advice is not always taken. We all live in that world. We don't have to imagine it. Murphy, you, me: we can all visualise what it must be to be Fauci, because we see it, on the television, in our social media feeds. We see an expert stranded by a post-truth regime, trying to summon help, signalling with his eyes. We understand the difference between us and him – and that is a hair's breadth.

For more than a decade in this country, the concern has been that we are sliding into a post-truth world, a place that renders shared reality an anachronism. The global financial crisis tipped the world into grievance. The digital disruption has amplified social divisions and polarisation. Grievance has been exploited by demagogues and media moguls intent on commodifying tribalism and conflict to attract paying audiences. Emotion, not reason, is the currency of loyalty. Loyalty to charlatans, like Trump. Loyalty to agents of cultural corrosion, like Fox News and its Australian mini-me, Sky News, where people pay to gather together as digital congregations to have their predispositions reinforced.

Because our experts and political leaders rallied to ensure we missed the worst of the economic shock in 2009, which gave birth globally to the politics of resentment, Australia has only flirted with the abyss. Sometimes our politics tips over the cliff face, and then it clambers back up. For a decade, I've watched, I've wondered, I've agonised – does Australia fall? When does it fall? It didn't fall after 2009, although our national politics descended into chaos for a decade. Is a 21st-century plague the moment?

All the fables of the plague canon suggest these crises are tipping points, when societies are consumed by the worst of their collective impulses.

Do we fall now, or do we refuse to fall?

That was the question at the beginning of this crisis. It still is.

THE IDES OF MARCH

Christian Porter remembers Friday the 13th of March vividly because the day ended with him believing he'd been infected with coronavirus and with his two small children crying loudly outside his office door. The attorney-general's memorably awful evening played out after he was told Peter Dutton, the home affairs minister, had tested positive to the coronavirus after a trip to the United States. Dutton and Porter sit next to each other during cabinet meetings, and had spent close to four hours on the Tuesday of that week trading their usual asides and banter at close range. Dutton says his COVID symptoms manifested early on Friday. Porter had his children with him in his Perth office when the bad news reached him. He is separated, and shares care of his children. The youngsters, two and four, were primed that they were coming to Dad's place, but Dutton's infection made that impossible. His wife came to collect them. As she closed the door behind them, he heard his children crying: "Where's Daddy? I thought we were going to be sleeping over at Daddy's house." He felt "tears in my soul" on two levels: "one about having my children crying because I had disappointed them because I wasn't taking them home that night, and the other one, which was I was going to be benched when I have been preparing to contribute at this point my whole life."

Porter didn't contract the virus, but Australia's management of COVID-19 did enter new territory that day. The Victorian and NSW premiers had their eyes trained on their health systems. Daniel Andrews and Gladys Berejiklian were worried Australia wasn't moving fast enough to mitigate the risks. As a consequence of those concerns, Australia was about to accelerate into a frenetic fortnight where swathes of the economy would be locked down and hundreds of thousands of people would lose their jobs.

Australia wasn't alone in this gear shift. As *The Economist* noted, the Ides of March weekend was when Europe woke up "to the sheer scale of the crisis it faced." The UK's Boris Johnson, who started lax, suddenly ordered people out of offices and pubs. Germany's Angela Merkel unveiled guidelines on physical distancing. Spain declared a state of emergency. Even Trump seemed to grasp fleetingly that this COVID thing might actually be bad.

Berejiklian and Andrews decided to assert themselves. Andrews had flagged his intentions three days earlier, when he told reporters gathered inside Royal Melbourne Hospital that "extreme measures" were coming. On Thursday, 12 March, at the prime minister's Sydney residence, Kirribilli House, the evening before the premiers were due to see Morrison for the Council of Australian Governments, Victorian officials told me, Andrews tried to convey the need for urgency to the prime minister when he lingered after the others left to have a drink. Morrison chuckles when I put that to him. "Dan and I had a scotch at Kirribilli. We were talking about something else." He wasn't trying to persuade you to hurry up on social distancing? "No, not at all. Not even remotely. We were talking about infrastructure. We talked about the economic package I'd just launched. That issue was brewing, but then, compared to now, it's chalk and cheese." Morrison said the main conversation at the leaders' dinner that night was about the need to stick together. "Dan and I were particularly of that view: that it would be very important. That was the key fusing."

On that Friday, the 13th, events were beginning to spiral. The world had reached 130,000 cases, with 4700 fatalities. Italy had recorded more than 1000 deaths. The health system there had been unable to cope with an influx of patients. Financial markets had been a mad roller-coaster for several days, but overnight Wall Street and London recorded their worst days since Black Monday in 1987. When local markets opened on 13 March, the Australian Securities Exchange plunged 7 per cent.

That day, the Australian leaders gathered, rather absurdly, in a cavernous empty football stadium in Parramatta, in western Sydney. The meeting began placidly with an economic update from the Treasury and the Reserve Bank of Australia, which focused on the negative impact of the bushfires on growth for the first quarter. The coronavirus was referenced in these briefings, but as a secondary issue. Brendan Murphy gave a briefing about COVID: according to an official in the room, the tone of the advice was that the outbreak was, of course, a significant concern, but things would get more worrying if community transmission escalated. The normal practice at COAG is that presentations are prepared days in advance, and then wind their way through cumbersome bureaucratic machinery.

Meeting alongside the political leaders was the AHPPC, and Murphy shuttled between the two groups. While the leaders' meeting was sailing along placidly, things were more robust in the health advisers' meeting. Victoria and New South Wales wanted social distancing restrictions imposed soon, so they dug in their heels. They wanted to ban large gatherings. Given the consensus in the group had obviously shifted in favour of more prompt and radical action, Murphy was forced to go back into the leaders' meeting and amend his medical advice. A note went in to Morrison.

People who know Murphy well say he's mastered the art of talking to politicians. But whatever Murphy's diplomatic skills, Morrison was deeply irritated by the change. Furious, say some. The prime minister says the reversal that day was the point in the crisis when he was most surprised. "Social distancing didn't become the discussion until about 2 p.m. … when I got the note from Brendan," he says.

The chief medical officer acknowledges that going back into the meeting of political leaders with a plan B went down like a lead balloon. "It was the famous day at Parramatta that we started to realise there was some very early community transmission, particularly in Sydney and a little tiny bit in Melbourne; there were cases appearing without clear known contacts that were being followed and isolated," Murphy says. He says the risks were elevated. "If you had any of those [cases], just one person going to a major gathering, we could see this was just starting. So we decided that we'd move quite early and start to put some bans on large gatherings." Murphy says that news came as "quite a shock to the premiers, but we needed to move relatively quickly. The first ministers were not too happy halfway through a meeting to get different information. But they said 'Okay, wish you'd told us earlier, but you've told us, so we'll act.'"

Morrison says he cleared the venue. This discussion would be leaders only. "I kicked everyone out of the room – my staff, every single official, every single premier's official – and I said to [the state and territory leaders], we need to deal with this as a team." Given the medical advisers in the two most populous states had just elected to change the tempo of the health response, the political leaders gathered in the football stadium needed to have a very frank conversation, peer to peer. The ad-hoc, unscripted huddle would war-game how to respond specifically to the health advice, and how to manage the crisis over the coming weeks and months. "We went around the room and the National Cabinet was born," Morrison says.

The prime minister created a new emergency government of nine to manage a national health crisis. Morrison suggested the "National Cabinet" title. The premiers and chief ministers wanted the group to be principals only, no Opposition leaders. At one level, this structure was just a rolling COAG meeting with a slightly grandiose title. At another level, it was a revolution in Australian governance. It was invented on the spot. No papers, no guidance from officials.

Morrison then had a specific problem he needed to resolve. He'd been signalling for much of the previous week his plan to go to the opening game of the NRL season, scheduled for Saturday night. But given the new health advice, leaders were now going to impose a ban on non-essential gatherings of 500 people. Would this ban be immediate? Wouldn't people need notice, given it was Friday afternoon? The inclination was to make the ban effective from Monday, not immediate. Morrison wondered out loud whether he should go the football or not. What message would he send if he did, given large crowd events were about to be banned? Conversely, would people be anxious if he suddenly said he wasn't going?

On the hop on that Friday, Morrison doubtless saw creating the National Cabinet framework as his best option. The Australian federation gives different tiers of government different responsibilities, and on that Friday it would have been obvious to everyone in the room that as things got tougher, and inevitably things would get tougher in a pandemic, leaders would start to blame-shift. Perhaps nobody in the room wanted the crisis to degenerate into a circular firing squad. Maybe you win the politics of that death match, maybe you don't.

While the raw political motive was pretty obvious – better deliberating together than brawling and duck-shoving in public, best we co-opt our traditional opponents and suspend the dynamics of partisanship and parochialism for mutual self-interest – there was also a practical objective. The states run hospitals and schools. The Commonwealth has primary responsibility for economic management. COVID-19 was a health emergency with profound economic implications. The only way to pull a response together and make it national and, where possible, uniform would be to create a structure to centralise decision-making.

This emergency government of nine, the National Cabinet, would be constituted as a sub-committee of the federal cabinet. In practical terms, this allows a group of leaders to deliberate and work quickly without much conventional democratic accountability. The National Cabinet is a top-down structure allowing the prime minister to determine an agenda, to deliberate in secret with the premiers and chief ministers, and to exercise power, potentially without much parliamentary oversight, and largely outside the limited reach of Australia's already anaemic freedom-of-information regime. It is a significant centralisation of power in the federation. This is the realpolitik of the shift, and Morrison likes what he sees. "The reason the National Cabinet works is because it is leader-led. COAG just sort of seeped everywhere. Leaders had to give this focus, direction and tasking."

The leaders have resolved that this structure will continue in perpetuity, in the world beyond the pandemic. There have been some adjustments. At the onset of the crisis, the National Cabinet was, as Morrison puts it, "just us and the AHPPC making decisions four times a week and telling health ministers and treasurers and everyone else to just get it done." Morrison later brought some of his line ministers back into the mix to help plan the post-COVID recovery. Not doing that would leave the prime minister open to internal griping about his actual cabinet being marginalised. It is unclear how the premiers will manage those same internal pressures down the track – what happens when ministerial colleagues in the states start becoming restive about lost influence? It is also unclear whether the hybrid kitchen cabinet of premiers and some ministers will become a source of internal tension for Morrison with his cabinet colleagues in time.

Morrison doesn't see a problem, at least not for him. He repeats that the weakness of COAG has been "the agenda, its objectives, have all percolated up, but I think leaders have to set the agenda for it, with tasks and timelines." He says the frequency of meetings is important. Holding meetings virtually is another plus, because no one feels they have to grandstand, or make bold declarations upon entering enemy territory. "The technology is also important because no one is turning up at a meeting and having a microphone put under their nose. They don't then have to engage in parochial wars, they just turn up and address a national agenda. One of the reasons it worked is everyone got out of their normal places on politics. Everyone accepted a national responsibility and they focused on it. I think [the premiers] quite liked that, actually."

In the opening months of the crisis, the National Cabinet allowed Morrison to muzzle the more ideological voices inside the Coalition. Running an emergency COVID-19 government in conjunction with the premiers kept Australia's pandemic response practical. It also suspended the usual conventions of partisan conflict. With state Labor premiers working in an emergency government with Morrison, the federal Opposition was both marginalised by the process and constrained to a degree by the cooperative participation of Labor premiers. There were a bunch of tasks to manage, and those tasks created the rationale for Morrison and his government to shape-shift. If public health required suspension of normal economic activity, then the need for a massive fiscal intervention was obvious, rather than an arcane ideological debating point.

If we distil 13 March down its the essence, Morrison formed a governing coalition with the premiers and chief ministers. The ad-hoc cabinet of leaders became of equal, if not greater, importance than his own cabinet, particularly in the opening couple of months. It also rendered the National Party, the unruly and increasingly rudderless governing partner in the federal Coalition, a total irrelevance.

In the longer term, there are pluses and minuses to this change in governance. The risks the premiers face over the longer term is co-option, becoming a branch office of the Morrison government. What happens over the long term, when the serious disagreements over the funding of services start? Some of this fractiousness is already visible. What happens, too, when leaders don't agree on the post-COVID reform program Morrison wants? Does the experiment end?

On the plus side, the innovation did shock COAG out of the purposeless rut it had been marooned in for the last few years, where it had presented to the world as a forum where proposals went to die. It instantly broadened Morrison's circle of political advice. Labor leaders suddenly found themselves part of the prime minister's inner sanctum, and in the early days of the crisis, when people were deeply anxious, the projection of a government of national unity was no bad thing. Geographic spread was also helpful. The challenges of managing COVID-19 are variable depending on the location, and the states and territories run services on the ground, which furnishes sharper insights.

While part of the purpose of the government of nine was secrecy and solidarity in deliberations, the spectrum of views, and the differing appetites for risk inside National Cabinet, would also force important conversations and deliberations into the open that otherwise would have occurred entirely out of public view. Over the next ten days, Australians would see that dynamic play out in spectacular fashion.

"MATE, LOCKDOWN IS COMING"

The week that followed the roller-coaster day in Parramatta saw an acceleration in social distancing restrictions. Two further meetings of the new National Cabinet resolved to ban cruise ships from docking, ban non-essential indoor gatherings of more than 100 people, and require all returning travellers to self-isolate for fourteen days upon arrival in Australia. Australians were told to limit their visits to aged-care facilities to protect a vulnerable cohort. Cinemas, theatres, restaurants and cafes, pubs and clubs were told they needed to be able to maintain 1.5 metres between patrons. Tasmania and the Northern Territory invoked state-based border controls on top of the national self-isolation requirements. Anyone entering either Tasmania or the Territory, even from another Australian state or territory, would have to self-isolate for fourteen days.

Thursday, 19 March, opened with news that Qantas would stand down two-thirds of its workforce and ground international flights. Later that day, Morrison broadened the travel ban, shutting the national border, walling Australia off from the rest of the world, in an effort to curtail the imported cases of COVID-19, which comprised 80 per cent of the caseload at that time. On the same day, the Reserve Bank of Australia made an emergency rate cut and flagged a $100 billion intervention into the financial system. Morrison and key ministers were also working flat-out on a second major economic stimulus package in as many weeks.

Things were moving so fast it was becoming impossible to stay ahead of the news, but Berejiklian and Andrews believed there was still more to do. Both were inclined to lock down non-essential services. The NSW premier had endured a terrible few days. Now that Australians were grasping that COVID-19 was more than a flu, parents were starting to panic about whether they should be sending their children to classrooms, and teachers through their unions were also applying pressure to close schools in the two most populous states.

That week saw the debacle of the *Ruby Princess*. On the Thursday, more than 2700 people were allowed to disembark from the cruise ship at Sydney's Circular Quay, despite more than 150 cases of illness being logged onboard. This was an appalling bungle, triggering hundreds of COVID-19 infections and eventually sparking a criminal investigation. As well as the lapses at the state level, Australian Border Force officials were later found to have played a role in not preventing disembarkations but an inquiry by Bret Walker QC cleared the ABF of responsibility for "the mishap." Compounding the *Ruby Princess* problem, hundreds of people flocked to Bondi Beach on the Friday evening and on the Saturday, ignoring the daily homilies about the importance of social distancing, and taking advantage of beautiful, mild early-autumn weather. The *Ruby Princess* and the mass "you only live once" assembly at Bondi were potent symbols: this pandemic was not under control. People were not getting the public health messages, and institutions needed to be sharpened up to deal with the risks.

As this was playing out, Craig Laundy was trying to come to terms with the rapidly changing regulatory environment in his family business, hotels. Laundy, a former Liberal cabinet minister, had left federal politics in 2019, repelled by the winner-takes-all culture of Canberra. Managers in his pubs were feeding up intelligence that as soon as they moved furniture to thin out the crowds in the bars, patrons would move it back again and congregate in close proximity. They were at their wits' end trying to manage the distancing rule of 1.5 metres. Laundy's former chief of staff in Canberra, Neil Harley, had remained in politics. He'd shifted to Macquarie Street and was now Berejiklian's chief of staff. Laundy thought he'd give Harley that feedback, and he gave the same intelligence to some old associates in Canberra, texting the MPs he knew were close to Morrison: Ben Morton, a West Australian Liberal Morrison calls "the apprentice," and Steve Irons, another pal of the prime minister.

"I had a phone conversation with Neil Harley on the Friday," Laundy recalls. "The [guidance about] one and a half metres had come in on the Wednesday. We straightaway reacted and did what we needed to do, but the accompanying guidelines and enforcement regime wasn't published until the Friday. On the Friday, I rang Neil to tell him we were finding the regime hard to enforce because we distance the furniture, we move it, and people just move it back." Laundy says he wasn't particularly alarmed about COVID at that point. "I was in the camp of some of us will get it and of course we should lock up the over-seventies – with a 79-year-old dad I was extremely worried about him – but I thought we youngsters, the word at that stage was you get it and you get better." But Harley's apocalyptic tone put the fear of God into him. "Neil Harley was my COS for four years and he is a very calm operator. He is very shrewd. He never gets into a panic. But he scared me. He said, 'Mate, lockdown is coming. I'm sorry. You have no idea what we are seeing – what is going on around the world.'" Laundy was taken aback. "I thought, wow. Neil was cool, calm and collected. He said, 'Mate, this thing, it is absolutely horrible, and we need to win.' I basically hung up from him on that Friday and I rang Dad and said to him, do nothing, get home now, we will bring you groceries – you are not going anywhere."

The Treasury secretary, Steven Kennedy, also knew lockdowns were coming because he'd been present at some of the conversations between his political masters in Canberra and the premiers. Understanding what was around the corner, Kennedy's strong advice to the government was to put a safety net in place through the social security system.

The National Cabinet was due to meet again the following Tuesday, after Morrison had unveiled his second stimulus package over the weekend. But Andrews, Berejiklian and Andrew Barr, the chief minister of the Australian Capital Territory, urged Morrison to bring the meeting forward to Sunday. As Harley had telegraphed to Laundy, the disposition in the populous states had shifted in favour of lockdowns. Barr was onboard because he felt there could not be one rule in Canberra and another in Queanbeyan – the town of 30,000-odd people just over the border in New South Wales.

Barr told me a few weeks after the tumultuous ten days in March that leaders were working frantically, and often cooperatively, but they were yet to synchronise their responses properly. As a result, they were lagging behind the curve of the pandemic. "We are getting there now, but we weren't quite there initially around fully appreciating how much the health curve would impact on the economic outcome," Barr says. "I think that gap is now being closed. There's been a few things that in hindsight you would like to have got there a week to ten days earlier, but we have got there – sometimes just in time."

Before the second wave hit his state in July, Daniel Andrews put the March scramble this way: "No one will benefit if this gets away from us, either in terms of lives lost, costs incurred or the massive impact that that would have on business." The Victorian premier said that over the course of March there was productive tension between the tiers of government about health outcomes and managing the economic shock accompanying the pandemic. "There is that tension, that's perfectly healthy and appropriate. It's a big thing to close businesses and see people stood down. These are massive decisions to make and there is a very big toll that comes with that, including anxiety and all sorts of other issues, often tragic issues, like increased family violence rates, for instance, and all sorts of other mental-health considerations. It's not a bad thing that we are all grappling with those very difficult choices."

To ensure they were on the same page about what needed to happen, Andrews and Berejiklian spoke several times during the day on Saturday. The NSW premier then told Morrison on Saturday evening that she wanted to impose stage one restrictions, which meant closing venues like pubs and clubs. If Morrison and the other premiers rebuffed them, the two premiers were prepared to go it alone.

On Sunday, 22 March, the number of COVID-19 cases in Australia sprinted past 1000. Morrison unveiled the $66-billion second stimulus package in Canberra – which boosted the safety net, as Kennedy had advised – and the prime minister also appeared to flag the broad direction the National Cabinet would be heading after the meeting later that day. During his press conference, Morrison pointed to the changes to come, flagging more "extreme measures" and localised lockdowns. He said governments had learnt over that weekend that people were not heeding social distancing entreaties: "Inevitably, and I suspect soon, there will be need for, in particular locations, more extreme measures to be taken."

Reading between the lines, it looked like the prime minister had heeded the premiers' warning, but the wheels were already in motion. A Nine Network reporter relayed some breaking news with a question to Morrison: would the prime minister care to comment on a push by the premiers for a total shutdown of non-essential businesses? This was not news to Morrison, but it was news to the Canberra press pack, and to people watching live at home. All the assembled reporters shifted their gaze from Morrison to their phones in an instant, and there was a mad scramble to text contacts in the states to confirm whether or not this was true. Were they pushing for a full Italian-style lockdown? The prime minister knew reporters were now chasing the next story, not focused on the $66 billion worth of stimulus, and he was irritated. Morrison noted crisply if he had anything to say about restrictions, he'd be saying it to the premiers later that day in an "orderly and calm" fashion.

Sunday had opened at a frantic pace, but over the coming hours events would accelerate. Victoria reported sixty-seven new cases and New South Wales ninety-seven, including eighteen infections linked to the *Ruby Princess*. The South Australian premier, Steven Marshall, stood up in Adelaide after the Morrison press conference and ordered the effective closure of the state border. As of 4 p.m. the following Tuesday, border control stations would be set up at the airport, at train stations and on roads entering the state. Western Australia followed suit. Berejiklian and Andrews publicly confirmed the push for lockdowns. The Victorian premier then upped the ante even further by saying he would close schools the following Tuesday.

That Sunday, I'd been plugged in to the news cycle from 6.30 a.m. because I was appearing on the ABC's *Insiders* program before beginning my day's work for *Guardian Australia*, where I am political editor. I'm generally calm when the news cycle is hectic – not because I have a magnificent zen-like temperament, but because anxiety in those circumstances wastes energy. I work in the white-water of 24/7 digital news: wasting energy is an unaffordable luxury. But that day, the unrelenting bedlam and the encroachment of the pandemic's rigid alternate reality – the reality where anxiety was the new normal – set my teeth on edge. Anxiety always needs a focal point, so when I wasn't pounding the keyboard or demanding various people confirm facts that were yet to be determined, I was fretting about my daughter.

She'd come to Canberra with a crew of fellow film-school graduates from Sydney to shoot a short film, but the production was quickly shut down because of COVID. Given the accelerating border closures, I was concerned she may have either to relocate back to Sydney sooner than she'd planned or dig in at home for the duration.

I probably alarmed her by phoning until she picked up and then demanding she turn on the news to make sure she was across the latest developments. Colleagues from other bureaus were walking off their nervous energy in the press gallery corridor between filing updates. Most of us hadn't had a proper day off for weeks, and were succumbing to gibberish. People were musing about whether it was possible to shut the border between the ACT and New South Wales, and mourning the abrupt end of the AFL season – another of Sunday's barrage of announcements.

Morrison, still clearly irritated by the day's events, did a round of prerecorded television interviews early on Sunday evening. Presumably these were pre-booked to sell the stimulus, but now all the curly questions were about lockdown, which had not yet been resolved.

Later that night, after the National Cabinet meeting, Morrison emerged in the Blue Room in Parliament House with a shopping list of changes. From midday Monday, clubs, hotels and pubs, cinemas, casinos and nightclubs would all close. Restaurants and cafes would be restricted to takeaway only. Indoor sporting venues and places of worship would close. Enclosed spaces for funerals and "things of that nature" would have to follow a strict four-square-metre rule, which would be enforced.

The centrepiece of Sunday's stimulus announcement – buried in the subsequent deluge – was an effective doubling of the Newstart unemployment payment. It was all too timely. Given the governments of Australia had just signed off on locking down large sections of the services economy, hundreds of thousands of people were about to lose their jobs. The next day the online government portal would crash and thousands of Australians would be lined up outside Centrelink in scenes reminiscent of the Great Depression.

During the first wave, I asked the treasurer, Josh Frydenberg, to identify the point he'd been most worried during the crisis. Apart from settling the anxious verbalisations of his five-year-old, who became very focused on "the virus, the virus, the virus – you can't catch the virus," Frydenberg's recollection was clear.

Later in the year, through July and August, the second wave in Victoria would keep the treasurer up at night. The disaster in his home state, the collapse in morale among friends and associates, and the economic impact of the second shutdown would eclipse all previous worries. But early in the crisis, his anxiety had a clear focus.

"My most worrying time was the long queues outside Centrelink," he said.

In newsrooms, editors are inclined on big days – leadership spills, ministerial reshuffles, resignations and the like – to ask Canberra reporters for quick pen portraits of the protagonists. After Malcolm Turnbull was blasted out of the prime ministership and Josh Frydenberg survived the defenestration with a promotion, the *Guardian*'s then economics writer, Gareth Hutchens, was charged with writing the 600-word Frydenberg pen portrait. I remember this vividly because Gareth asked me if he could start the piece with an anecdote about a parachute. I thought this was mad, until I heard the story, which was perfect. It went like this. A few years ago, a young skydiver survived a 4000-metre fall after his parachute failed and he landed on soft ground. Lying in hospital afterwards with a broken back, he said the freak experience wasn't pleasant, but he was "trying to focus on the positives." This is Australia's treasurer in two sentences. Somehow, survive the fall that would kill anyone else, then focus on the positives, because otherwise you miss opportunities.

Before Turnbull was felled by the right, he deployed Frydenberg to help him land his final attempt to persuade the Liberal Party to adopt an energy policy with an emissions-reduction component. The treasurer said the attempt to put together the National Energy Guarantee during a leadership crisis was good training for managing the economic shock of a pandemic. "When I went through the NEG, that vortex – it's not similar to coronavirus, but the intensity of those big policy battles and public battles, prepares you, it helps build resilience. That's helpful at times like this." Frydenberg in his youth harboured an ambition to be a professional tennis player. "It's like when you are training for something, if you haven't pushed yourself or been pushed, once you get to game day your ability to respond as required is less likely to happen."

In the opening months of the crisis, the economic interventions were as important as the health response. Another key moment for Frydenberg was when he first understood COVID-19 was going to blow everything off-course. That realisation happened in Saudi Arabia. He went to Riyadh for a meeting convened by the International Monetary Fund in the third week of February.

Frydenberg's sharper awareness wasn't triggered by deft IMF forecasting. At that stage, the IMF was forecasting the negative impact of COVID-19 on the global economy would be only 0.1 per cent. China had told the meeting the outbreak was being controlled. But Singapore had struck a sombre note, predicting it would run a deficit to manage the pandemic. Singapore's negative tone caused a frisson.

At dinner Frydenberg sat with the Saudi hosts of the conference at a table with Steve Mnuchin, the American Treasury secretary. The Australian treasurer was seated next to the Italian representative, who had to take an urgent call during the meal. The Italian returned to the table and told Frydenberg the virus was spreading rapidly at home. He'd had to sign off on emergency health spending. The Italian told Frydenberg the number of cases had jumped significantly and the management of the crisis was becoming very difficult.

Frydenberg says the combination of the pessimism from Singapore and the frontline account from his Italian colleague helped him grasp the dimensions of what was still a creeping crisis. The Australian government's first economic stimulus package was out a mere two weeks later.

The previous July, Steven Kennedy was appointed Treasury secretary. Kennedy has an unusual background, beginning his professional life as a nurse before doing a PhD in economics. His doctoral thesis examined whether changes in economic outcomes had an impact on people's health. Kennedy these days wears the regulation well-tailored dark suits and rectangle-shaped glasses of the Treasury econocrat. He has a long, thin face, defined features, expressive hands, and a flick of sculpted brown hair that sweeps back off a high forehead from a side part. But there is something of the health professional still in the manner: call it a flicker of emotional intelligence. In addition to his service across several government departments, Kennedy had two stints serving Labor prime ministers, including working as an adviser on the macro-economy in Kevin Rudd's office during the global financial crisis. He was also integrally involved at the bureaucratic level in designing the emissions-trading scheme that was legislated by the Gillard government during the forty-third parliament. Kennedy has prospered under the Coalition despite possessing a background that hardliners would consider suspect.

Martin Parkinson, another senior bureaucrat who found himself on the wrong side of the carbon wars with the Coalition when Tony Abbott removed him from Treasury, famously lived to fight another day, ending his career as the head of the Department of Prime Minister and Cabinet. He recommended Kennedy for Treasury secretary. "He's got a first-rate intellect, it's not just good analytics, he understands how to win people over to positions," Parkinson says. "He's a real pragmatist. He understands politics, in particular the opportunities and boundaries that it creates. He knows how to work in a complex political environment while having really good clarity about what is first best policy."

Fortuitously, Kennedy had conducted research on the economic impact of a pandemic, his interest triggered by avian flu and SARS. Back in 2006, he was the lead author of a departmental working paper that had concluded that a highly contagious pandemic could knock 5 per cent off GDP during the first year. Kennedy's paper had some sharp take-outs for the government now charged with managing the response. The first was that even a well-contained pandemic killing a relatively small number of people would have a "large, short-run economic impact." It noted that "quickly re-establishing consumer and investor confidence is likely to be one of the important roles for governments to play." To achieve that goal, governments had a lever they could pull: "discretionary fiscal policy."

Morrison isn't known for having cuddly sentiments about public servants. Early in his tenure as prime minister, he sounded a public warning to Canberra's bureaucrats: governments make policy and public servants should set about delivering it. But Kennedy had the ear of both Morrison and Frydenberg, particularly early in the crisis. His advice was extremely influential in determining the government's economic response.

Some say he remains close to Frydenberg, but Morrison cooled on him after Treasury had to concede a significant forecasting error with the JobKeeper payment in late May. The prime minister denies that flatly. "Not at all," he says. "People have been outstanding. It has been the best of the public service; for many of them this has been their finest hour." Considering the error, which reduced the anticipated cost of the wage subsidy from $130 billion to $70 billion, Morrison says: "If you are going to hit the wrong side of the line, that was a better side of the line to hit." He says when Treasury prepared the forecast, the government was working on the worst case. "We were thinking about ICUs overwhelmed, a six-month lockdown. That all could have happened. The good news is it didn't."

Parkinson thinks the crisis has seen an evolution in the government's thinking about experts, and its preparedness to listen to advice from officials. "We'll do the thinking, you'll do the doing – that never works, but you might be able to delude yourself in thinking that it works in more normal times. In crises you need experts. To the government's eternal credit, they've recognised that and they've drawn on the expertise of the chief medical officer and his team for the medical response, and on Treasury and [Prime Minister and Cabinet] in formulating the economic policy response."

The eminent academic economist Bob Gregory, who knew Kennedy when he did his PhD, says Australia has been lucky to have him at the helm of Treasury. "We are going through absolutely extraordinary times, times where you shouldn't really trust the experts. By that I don't mean trust in that Trumpian sense, but I mean trust in the sense that they haven't experienced this before either." He says everyone made early predictions. Epidemiological experts predicted huge numbers of deaths from COVID-19 without referencing the huge number of deaths societies generally tolerate through other diseases, or from motor vehicle accidents.

> For example, in Australia in 2018 the flu epidemic was so bad that we had an extra 800 deaths that year. Nobody noticed.
>
> The experts can't be completely trusted. The same is true of economists. We are going into areas now where we are spending sums of money that no economist in their right mind would have ever dreamt of. So what this means is when the expert comes in and lays down the law, as you want them to do, you've got to say to yourself, this guy is an expert, he is very well trained, but I've still got to exercise judgment here because this is a such a weird set of events.

Gregory says Kennedy is a person not afraid to exercise that judgment in a high-stakes environment. "He's somebody who is open. I think Kennedy is open."

In late February and into early March, Frydenberg and Kennedy worked through the options for the first economic stimulus package. The conversation started with about fifteen measures, and then the options were whittled down. The contest evidently moved quickly. The finance minister, Mathias Cormann, declared on 6 March that the government would not be pursuing "a cash splash in the reckless Rudd–Gillard fashion." By 9 March, Frydenberg and Kennedy had resolved to craft a package worth close to 1 per cent of GDP, which would dispense cash to people with a high marginal propensity to consume – that meant money for people on income support. There was a lot of internal conversation about how to get the cash payment number right. The advice from Treasury was that people on income support would spend the money right away, whatever the prevailing conditions, and there was a pre-existing delivery mechanism through the tax and transfer system, which mitigated the risk of something going wrong. (The Coalition had spent years blasting Labor for sending cheques to dead people.)

While round one has faded into memory because it was quickly superseded by rounds two and three, resolving to embark on stimulus – even if the need for it was blindingly obvious – was a significant political turnaround for a government that had pilloried Labor's response to the global financial crisis for the best part of a decade. In order to set some boundaries around the jarring political reversal, Morrison wanted not to repeat any mistakes Labor had made. The former Labor minister Greg Combet, who had been drafted by the Coalition to help manage the labour-market elements of the crisis, counselled Morrison against creating new programs through the stimulus measures. Combet was speaking from painful experience: he'd had to clean up the pink batts scheme, which was part of the GFC stimulus measures.

As well as the cash payments, the first stimulus package also included a fund to support tourism and export businesses that had ground to a halt because of COVID. The minister for trade, tourism and investment, Simon Birmingham, had visited a number of regions to feed information back into the deliberations. In some regions, people were worried that mass unemployment and mass business failures would lead to civil unrest. "It was day after day of really heartbreaking conversations with people who have invested their lives in building businesses to show other people a great time," Birmingham recalls.

> The experience was as diverse as the Cairns Aquarium taking me through and visually seeing the amount of equipment, filtration plants, et cetera, required to run that business, that can't be switched off. It can't be mothballed in the sense of reducing costs at that level, and knowing that these types of businesses were going to need lifelines to be able to maintain their existence through the coming months, through to the tiny adventure speedboat operators who are Mum and Dad businesses, worried about their staff and the repayments due on the boats and how they could keep their infrastructure in place.

As well as the small operators, there were big companies in distress. "I had an ASX-listed company CEO tearing up across the table talking about what he thought would be the likely collapse of his major business and the regional repercussions if that was the case."

Birmingham says he was deeply unnerved by the first wave of frontline anxiety he was fielding. "For a period of time there, not knowing how successfully we were going to be able to respond, there was a degree of, not scared, but certainly deep, deep worry." The worry would hit him in his car. "I remember getting back to Adelaide. The only moments I had to stop and think about it were the moments I had in the car, driving on my own, to the office, and they were deeply depressing moments. The radio was relaying horrors of the health failures overseas and my mind was reverberating the horrors of the economic consequences that were bearing down on businesses and employees here." In the darker moments, Birmingham says he wondered whether there was actually a way through a problem as complex as the one the government faced, when every response to every problem created fresh challenges. Closing the borders and imposing social distancing restrictions felled the tourism industry, but there was no choice if the overarching objective was to flatten the curve of infections.

Christian Porter says there was another dimension to the anxiety the government felt at that time – it couldn't usefully compare its own policy responses with what was happening internationally. "Game theorists talk about follow-the-leader strategies, where there is safety in following the leader, but I don't think this was one of those environments where we could safely adopt that strategy. There were points where [we] had to be the first to do something and make that decision." I ask Porter whether the government couldn't compare Australian responses with the responses elsewhere because there were so many irrational actors on the world stage. I expect a diplomatic formulation, but he's candid. "Completely," the attorney-general says.

Birmingham acknowledges that it could have been difficult for the Coalition to abandon its avowed position on stimulus, but pragmatism won the day. "In the end, no. There was such a clear need that was emerging. The conversations we were all having with business and communities were consistent. Designing the solution was tough. The instincts initially were the right ones: that a whole new program and way of doing this would be slower and riskier, and simply scaling up existing programs was going to be a quicker way of delivering assistance." But he says the government knew as soon as round one was out the door that it wasn't enough. "We realised the gaps were too great and we needed to plug those gaps if we were to maintain productive capacity in the economy that was going to be necessary for the rebound. Stimulus one was classic stimulus and a determination not to repeat what we saw as the failings of previous stimulus in terms of creating new high-risk programs that were potentially wasteful." But the next stimulus had to address lockdowns across the services economy – hospitality, retail, tourism.

Kennedy's pandemic paper in 2006 hadn't countenanced lockdowns. It imagined more organic responses to a pandemic: consumers stop spending, workers in service industries stay at home because of concern about catching the illness, and disruptions to global trade flows. The paper predicted that investment and consumption would take a hit because of a fall in confidence, demand for exports would fall, "and some industries such as tourism and restaurants may virtually close down." But there was nothing virtual about the shutdowns being driven by the National Cabinet. As Birmingham puts it, because of the intensifying public health measures, the government was now looking at a "mass loss of work scenario." That was the intellectual core of the second stimulus package. The government of robodebt was about to shape-shift again in radical fashion.

We need to stop and remember just how remarkable it was that a government with an appetite to chase welfare debts so voraciously that it led to potential illegality would double the Newstart payment without breaking a sweat. But that is what happened on 22 March. The Coalition doubled income support and called the payment "JobSeeker."

After employers responded rationally to that development and sacked thousands of staff on 23 March, the government went back to the bunker and re-emerged seven days later with the biggest policy of all: a wage subsidy originally forecast to be worth $130 billion over six months. Josh Frydenberg's chief of staff suggested that it be called "JobKeeper." This was the forecast Treasury had to correct a couple of months later, costing the department some skin with Morrison. The wage subsidy would now cost the budget $70 billion.

The decision-making tempo was accelerating to keep pace with events – principals and officials were grinding through deliberations and decisions around the clock. "We didn't sleep much at that time," Morrison says. "The meetings went on for hours and hours and hours, because we were so conscious of not repeating the mistakes of the GFC." He says the core principles for the fiscal response were set by him, Frydenberg and Kennedy, and "they guided everything we did."

Morrison characterises the government's response as non-ideological conservatism – a concept we'll unpack in a bit – but for now, let's capture the dynamic inside the government, because it's important.

While Morrison and Frydenberg and the cabinet sub-committees were meeting around the clock, not everyone was happy with the direction of the economic response. On the Coalition backbench, frustration was rising. The government was changing its political identity in full public view, crafting a cascade of what many regarded as centre-left policy responses, and spending billions of dollars at a rapid pace, with only limited internal consultation.

The Rudd government famously ran into trouble when it narrowed the pathway for decision-making during the GFC. It was government by a "gang of four" – a streamlined methodology conceived in an emergency – but that decision-making style lingered for too long afterwards, stoking resentments that exploded when Rudd was driven out of the prime ministership. The downsides of keeping major decisions too close are now deep in Canberra's muscle memory.

Cabinet seems to have been in the loop even though the pace was frantic, and there were rolling meetings of its Expenditure Review Committee and National Security Committee – sometimes twice a day. These two committees are the engine room of any government, and they have certainly been the engine room during this crisis. Decisions would loop back into the full cabinet as general business, although when asked to recall whether all the decisions went back to the whole group, some senior players struggle to separate what they read in media reports from decisions they did or didn't take, because there were so many meetings and because events were unfolding so quickly.

As well as cabinet deliberations, there would normally have been briefings of backbench committees before major announcements. But the government's backbench economics committee did not see either the first or second stimulus packages before they were announced. If the doubling of the Newstart payment in stimulus two had gone through the usual internal processes, Morrison and Frydenberg would have faced questions about why it was happening. Some would have opposed the quantum of the increase, while others would have campaigned to extend support to other constituencies. A meeting of the backbench economics committee was scheduled for 23 March, the day after stimulus two was released. That meeting was cancelled. MPs began complaining either among themselves or to ministers directly about being out of the loop. "Particularly in those early weeks, they were finding all sorts of reasons why it was technically not feasible to have meetings to consider legislation, and to have questions asked on phone calls," one backbencher says.

There was also significant internal disquiet about the government's decision to provide free child care. That package was unveiled on 2 April. Some MPs were, as one puts it forcefully, "utterly bewildered" that a centre-right government was bankrolling free child care. Barnaby Joyce is the chair of the backbench education committee. The committee was convened after the package was announced and there was a short summary of the new measures before Joyce declared the package approved unless anyone had any major issues. No legislation or briefing paper was presented to the MPs to assess. Perhaps reflecting the reality that the policy lacked a critical mass of champions in the government, free child care would be one of the first supports to be wound back.

The government scheduled teleconferences during March to bring the party room along with the rapid-fire decision-making, but MPs say initially questions weren't welcomed, even though the software allowed people to register an intention to ask a question. Instead, MPs were told to submit their queries by email to Bronwyn Morris, the backbench liaison staffer in Morrison's office, and the prime minister would answer some of them. This effective vetting of queries didn't last. Later, the government reactivated the backbench committees, probably sensing that some of the arguments brewing behind the scenes would spill over into the public domain unless there was a circuit-breaker.

As the internal tensions heightened, Morrison also sharpened his public language about the "snap-back" – the point at which the stimulus would end – presumably with one eye on managing expectations from the public, and the other on maintaining internal equilibrium.

Possibly senior ministers weren't actively avoiding internal checks and balances. It is entirely possible, as one government figure put it to me candidly, they were just blindsided and "panicked" by an escalating crisis. The pace was "hysterical," another says with a chuckle. Time was of the essence. Time spent with colleagues explaining and cajoling was time that wasn't spent elsewhere, and the opportunity cost of every second during that period was carefully weighed.

As time passed, things improved. By the third round of stimulus, there were two teleconferences with the backbench economics committee. The first was on 1 April, shortly after the wage subsidy had been unveiled. A second meeting was scheduled for 3 April, but that was delayed until late afternoon on Sunday, 5 April, because the necessary legislation wasn't yet ready to consider. That legislation was circulated only an hour before the meeting, which caused some angst.

As we saw earlier, the treasurer's most anxious time during the pandemic was triggered by the queues outside Centrelink that began on Monday, 23 March. Less surprised about the Centrelink queues was Sally McManus, the ACTU secretary.

Ex-Labor MP Greg Combet had advised Christian Porter, who holds the industrial relations portfolio as well as being attorney-general, to bring McManus in to help manage the labour-market impacts of the pandemic. Porter had appointed Combet as a consultant on 20 March. He knew he needed conduits into the union movement to help him manage a truce, and weighed up whether Combet or another Labor man, Simon Crean, would be better for the task. He resolved to appoint Combet, with Morrison's backing. The negotiated truce was necessary because Porter and the labour movement had been brawling for months over the government's Ensuring Integrity Bill, which proposed to tighten regulations covering unions and officials. Porter wanted to lay down the cudgels, so he phoned McManus on Combet's advice, and also senior officials of the Construction, Forestry, Maritime, Mining and Energy Union, and declared the old arguments were "on pause." "Saving jobs – that was the only issue that was important, everything else was on hold," Porter says. "Nothing else mattered."

McManus reciprocated. At the first meeting she attended with Porter and employer groups, she told her fellow attendees that trade unions were "prepared to put aside everything and work together" to save incomes and jobs. Scott Morrison phoned her after that meeting to thank her for the collegiality. McManus remembers taking that call on 21 March because she was at a memorial service for a colleague and had to duck out discreetly to answer it, wandering a suburban street in Melbourne talking to the prime minister on WhatsApp.

Morrison would unveil the doubling of Newstart the next day. McManus says she warned the government that would trigger mass layoffs from the moment she was invited to the table. McManus wasn't opposed to increasing income support, but knowing something of labour-market dynamics, her working supposition was that many employers would wash their hands of staff if the government doubled the safety net. The JobSeeker payment, while entirely well-intentioned, sent a message to employers "that they could let staff go and they would be looked after."

Morrison boosted the safety net on Sunday, the day that the premiers won their pitched battle for the partial lockdown of pubs and clubs. Restaurants were pared back to takeaway outlets. Business owners had been jolted, and gained the impression that Australia was hurtling inexorably towards an Italian-style lockdown of all non-essential services.

The mass sackings started from first light on Monday, 23 March. "I think that really shook the government," McManus says. What followed, she says, was "forty-eight hours of total carnage for us. We had workers stood down and laid off all over the place." Over those days, Porter tracked two sets of data: stand-downs under section 524 of the *Fair Work Act*, and applications for unemployment benefits. "What was unbelievably clear is they weren't a smooth bunch of applications," Porter recalls. "An event would happen, so information or data would hit the marketplace and people would respond, and so for both Sally and I, the day where we had hundreds of thousands, I think 400,000 people in a day, apply for welfare just crystallised what we'd both been talking about – that job saving was the only issue of any real importance."

Craig Laundy says those first few days of lockdown were chaos. The initial advice from the Australian Hotels Association was to terminate all casual employees. "It was a scramble for information," he says. "We didn't know what to do with full-time[rs] and part-timers for the first three or four days, but we did know we had to terminate the casuals. I think we did that on March 23. We terminated our casuals first up and prepared to stand down our full-timers. The casuals went straight to Centrelink, and it was very clear from day one that Centrelink was not geared to deal with mass unemployment." Laundy says when JobKeeper followed a week later, he tracked down the casuals who were eligible and re-engaged them, so they could get access to the $1500 payment.

McManus says she was determined to convince the government to develop a wage subsidy, so that workers wouldn't lose the connection to their places of employment. "We already were pushing the wage subsidy argument, but after that happened we thought every ounce of our energy had to go into winning this. If we didn't win it, we would see a generation of mass unemployment." The key to winning, she thought, was to make sure the key business groups became advocates, and "one by one, employer groups came on board."

Treasury moved on to designing the next round of stimulus immediately after JobSeeker was unveiled. The flipside of the criticisms levelled by McManus is that the doubling of the Newstart payment meant there was now a decent safety net to cushion people during the worst of the economic shock. Some officials contend Treasury pushed the social security change ahead of the larger wage subsidy deliberately, to make sure the vulnerable had income support. When Kennedy appeared before a Senate inquiry, he said it was his advice to get the safety net in place first before doubling back with the larger wage subsidy that was unveiled on 30 March. Morrison says Kennedy's advice reflected the sequence the prime minister wanted. "We wanted the safety net before the wage subsidy, that needed to come first, because that's what everyone was going to fall [back] on." He said he wasn't ever opposed to wage subsidies, he just didn't like the version that had been rolled out by Boris Johnson in the United Kingdom, where workers would be paid 80 per cent of their salary. In advice given to Frydenberg on 21 March, Treasury identified flaws in the British model, including that it gave more generous support to higher-income earners than those on low incomes. "We worked on our own until we hit the right model," Morrison says. Frydenberg is adamant that a wage subsidy was always on the table.

While the prime minister anticipated some public resistance to a wage subsidy, and Kennedy at that point was working up alternatives, including PAYG tax relief options to support employers, the government understood that a third stimulus package would be required. Birmingham says stimulus three addressed the fact that "there was a real and present danger to the recovery if we didn't keep people attached to business, and we needed to address business failure as much as possible." Advisers pitched an Australian version like this: JobKeeper would be another form of liquidity for businesses disrupted by the pandemic – a massive injection to the balance sheet that would flow through to employees. The wage subsidy would be a mechanism to support parts of the economy where people would have a prospect of remaining employed after the pandemic. The government wanted to use existing delivery mechanisms for the stimulus programs, not reinvent the wheel – and what better existing mechanism than the wages system? A wage subsidy would be an alternative form of social security payment, using the payroll as the delivery mechanism.

Laundy, a former workplace minister, thinks the government chose to engage the Tax Office to handle the wage subsidy payments once it became obvious Centrelink wasn't geared up for mass lay-offs. "The ATO has an ongoing relationship with every employer in the country and every staff member of every employer. They have relationships across the board because everyone has to register for tax file numbers. They know basically just short of what size shoe you are – so I reckon the government outsourced the functionality of Centrelink effectively to the employers in the country. That outsourcing is called JobKeeper." I consider this a working theory of Laundy's – speculation from the sidelines – until I hear the idea come out of Morrison's mouth. "We effectively privatised the social security system into corporate payrolls," he says. "That's exactly what we did. If we didn't roll out JobKeeper, all those people would have been on

Centrelink queues within a day and the entire social security system would have collapsed under the strain. It was very important."

The government took the decision to implement a wage subsidy on the evening of 26 March. The core principles were drafted in a meeting that Morrison squeezed in before participating in a teleconference of G20 leaders just before midnight. Present were Morrison, Frydenberg and finance minister Mathias Cormann, as well as Kennedy and Treasury deputy secretary Jenny Wilkinson.

Earlier that day, during a background briefing with journalists, Morrison floated the conceptual framework guiding the policy-making. Frydenberg talked about the economy being cryogenically frozen. Morrison talked about a "hibernation" strategy. One official believes that particular characterisation may have actually originated with one of the premiers, rather than the prime minister or the treasurer, but in any case, the hibernation strategy was explained like this. If there was no demand, because public health required a partial shutdown of the economy, the government wanted to work with businesses, banks, insurers and regulators to engineer a situation where employers could enter a period of suspended animation – essentially their costs, liabilities, rents and other outgoings would be frozen for the lockdown period so that businesses could emerge on the other side without having accumulated liabilities so substantial that they would sink them. Part of the hibernation strategy was a wage subsidy tying workers to their employers.

Once they'd resolved to go, Frydenberg told Kennedy and Wilkinson JobKeeper had to be a "break glass" moment. He meant it needed to be big enough to boost confidence. People would criticise the subsidy if it wasn't commensurate with a replacement wage in the hardest-hit sectors, such as retail and hospitality. He wanted options about the level of payment to consider. "We were looking at all options. We were looking at an amount that was similar to the JobSeeker payment. Obviously, some people had publicly commented that it should be the median wage. There were lots of different options. Fifteen hundred dollars [per fortnight] is about

70 per cent of the median wage. It was a significant amount of money, and, importantly, in the sectors hardest hit it would be as close to a median wage as you can get."

Cabinet's expenditure review committee rolled forward into near-continuous meetings until final sign-off. There were queries from colleagues about the $1500 figure. Was it appropriate that some workers would receive a pay rise? The advice was that the economic benefit of the ensuing stimulus would outweigh the downsides of a taxpayer-funded pay rise – and it was simpler to give part-time workers with more than one employer a single payment rather than a bunch of smaller payments through different employers. There were also concerns about the astronomical price tag in the forecast: $130 billion in six months.

Morrison says the pay rise was a deliberate feature of the policy. The overpayment of people "was very deliberate, because we knew we couldn't put everybody in it. While people may have been paid more by that employer under JobKeeper, they probably lost their other job or two jobs, which means effectively we were getting one employer to cover off for the second job. That was important. This was a more efficient way of delivering income support and we were prepared to wear that as the price of simplicity."

Frydenberg says he gulped when he saw the final number. Journalists weren't quite so delicate. When the number was unveiled on 30 March, the reporter standing next to me squeaked, "Fuck!", before trying to swallow the involuntary outburst. Presumably after hearing similar sentiments expressed by their political masters, Treasury officials reassured nervous ministers the expenditure was both manageable and necessary.

The Treasurer also consulted major employers in the relevant sectors in the hope that obvious bugs could be spotted in advance of the formal announcement, but there were a number of problems with the scheme that persisted for months. Peter Burn, the director of policy at Ai Group, says there were "more than a small number of issues" with JobKeeper at the start, ranging from initial slowness on the part of the ATO in deeming employers eligible for the scheme to the lack of incentives for lower-paid people to work extra hours. "Overall, the problems arose because it was developed quickly, there was no time for consultation. Nothing could be done about that. It had to be delivered quickly." The government and the bureaucracy were fully extended, but they were still running behind events. The support packages were coming, and coming fast when you consider the sedate pace at which governments normally move. But crises always move faster. Crises are nimble, and light on their feet. It also took time for the government to comprehend just how deep its pockets needed to be. It took time to accept that a short, sharp downturn and a V-shaped recovery wasn't the most likely scenario.

As well as teething problems with the hastily designed JobKeeper, there was the simpler matter of who was left outside the net deliberately, either for cost reasons or because of politics. Casuals who had worked for their employers for less than twelve months found themselves ineligible for the payment. Nor were most workers on temporary visas included. Universities were marooned outside the net, and furious about it, given the travel bans that had deprived them of international fee-paying students. The government says it carved universities out because it was dealing with their woes through separate support packages – but the sector was likely excluded to try to contain the cost of the program. There is also a view in some quarters of the Coalition that universities are factories of left-wing thought. Including universities in the rescue would have been controversial for some members of the government.

While the fundamentals of the wage subsidy were now in place, a delicate period lay ahead in the rapprochement between the government and the unions. While McManus was one of the voices championing a wage subsidy, implementing it would require opening up the *Fair Work Act*. Porter says as the options were worked through, it became clear to his advisers and accepted by Treasury that JobKeeper wouldn't work unless the government changed the law. The advice was that a third of the scenarios where you might see the $1500 apply would be unlawful because people were receiving less than what they were normally paid. Opening up the underpinning legislation would be the thin edge of the wedge for the ACTU. Porter says he had to work respectfully. "I had to make it clear I wasn't going to use this as an opportunity to tick off some 1990s IR wishlist when I opened the Act up, which required an enormous amount of trust."

When Porter broached the subject, McManus responded predictably. She made it clear she wanted to deal with the potential illegalities by adjusting awards and workplace agreements, not by changing the legislation. But he says she left the door open to negotiate. Porter brought in Combet to help him manage the cross-currents.

> He was helping us think down the track, he understands how legislation works, he understands how legislative processes work. He's the best lawyer non-lawyer I've come across – he's just got it.
>
> Combet helped in that process from the very first draft. I didn't have the luxury of starting with drafting instructions and drafting principles and then sending them off to the Office of Parliamentary Counsel. We worked on a draft with external lawyers and this office ourselves, and when we got it into a shape that we thought was acceptable we sent it down to OPC to redraft in their inimitable Commonwealth style.
>
> But Greg was watching the drafts and said this won't fly, this will scare people, this could easily be opened to misuse, this would be a weakness in the way it would be administered. He's got a great cautionary radar for these things. So, at about draft 15 we were at the point we could truly say we had a working draft. I went to Sally and we were literally on the phone arguing the toss about line-by-line drafting.

McManus says there were conflicts, but by then she'd formed a foundational level of trust with Porter. "He didn't play games. He just tries to deal practically with what he has in front of him. We are used to dealing with right-wing governments looking to find what advantage they can press with you, but there's been none of that, and none of that on our side either."

Porter's assessment is similar. "There's a lot of trust. We've dealt with each other under intensely difficult circumstances and there's been nothing done or said to lead me to believe that Sally can be taken at anything other than her word. If she says she's going to do something, she does it, if she says she won't provide information to another person, that information is not provided to another person." There is trust, he says, "but our worldviews are seriously different."

Given this, I ask McManus whether the reset in the relationship will last. "My experience, going through crisis – the union movement is used to crises, that's what we deal with, everything from the MUA dispute to Ansett – relationships, or an understanding of someone, that might normally take three years to get to can happen in three months, because you see people at their best and their worst. You learn who you can actually trust when the stakes are high."

Will this goodwill persist after COVID, when the government will pursue more radical industrial relations changes to kickstart the economy? Can a bond of trust between a union leader and an industrial relations minister survive the Coalition's wish-list for labour-market deregulation? It seems unlikely. "What I'm saying is, I think things will change," McManus says. "It's not possible to say to what extent, or whether it will be long-lasting."

The opening months of the crisis pushed principals and their advisers to the limits of endurance and policy ingenuity. But the really hard decisions, the ones that will define who we are as a consequence of this event, are all before us. The hardest work is not behind the government and the community; it is in front of us. Morrison knows that, which is why this essay began with his answer to that question.

Before the former Liberal senator Arthur Sinodinos left Australia to take up his post as Australia's ambassador to the United States, he gave me a couple of helpful organising thoughts about Scott Morrison. The first was that this prime minister is at ease with all aspects of the job. Not all PMs are. But Morrison, who came to politics via the party organisation, likes it all: the backroom stuff; the anatomy of the campaign, which some prime ministers leave to their strategists; the research; the shaping of messages.

Everybody who knows Morrison well encourages me to think of him as a prime minister who maintains the mindset of a party director. In the Liberal Party, directors are trouble-shooters. They fix problems. The mindset is about winning and creating pathways to victory. Get the experts in, get the finance people in, get the pollster in, and war-game the problem. Morrison doesn't rhapsodise about "reform." At his core, he's a populist, and a fixer, not an ideologue. He finds shibboleths, the core philosophical mantras of some of his centre-right predecessors and contemporary colleagues, boring, tired, tedious, claustrophobic. Party directors are project managers, and it is helpful to think of Morrison as a project manager rather than the keeper of an ideological flame.

Morrison in 2017, when he was still treasurer, defined the project of the contemporary Liberal Party. Never lacking confidence, Morrison took his new definition right to the heart of his political organisation, the Liberal Party's federal council, a year after Malcolm Turnbull scraped home in the 2016 election. He told fellow travellers they couldn't keep living off past glories. The party had to become the Liberal Party of the post-GFC world.

Slavishly following orthodoxies was out. "Australians have their own tribes, which usually have nothing to do with politics, and their views do not always fit neatly into our partisan boxes, and nor do they care." He said the post-GFC voter was frustrated and disempowered economically, and suspicious about whether systems worked for them. "Thick ice" separated the political class and the average person. People wanted to be listened to and they wanted results. Morrison's populist instincts came to the fore when he defined the two questions at large in Australian society: do you get it, and are you on my side? "The challenge for us as Liberals is to come to terms with the fact that it is no longer about convincing Australians to be on our side, but to convince Australians that we are on theirs."

Sinodinos had two other prescient observations about how Morrison's prime ministership would go. The first was that events would intrude, because prime ministers now govern nations in a globalised world. One of his primary lessons serving John Howard was that external shocks take up huge amounts of time and prime ministerial energy. The second observation was the lack of perfect information informing major decisions; prime ministerships are as much art as science. "Politics is an ambiguous environment, where you have to make all sorts of choices with incomplete information. There's an X-factor, issues emerge from left field, and you have to deal with them." As the economist Bob Gregory has argued, experts get you a distance, but they only get you so far.

Morrison would like Australians to think COVID-19 is the first significant crisis of his prime ministership, because the case study serves as the exemplar. His response to the pandemic wasn't perfect. He was too slow at the beginning, and he wasn't always coherent. Not enough was done to safeguard the aged-care sector – a Commonwealth responsibility. Those deficiencies became clearer during the second wave.

But in general terms Morrison rose to the occasion, so let the record show the prime minister passed his first major test. Except his first major test wasn't COVID, it was the bushfires of December and January, and then the prime minister did not rise to the occasion. His Midas touch completely deserted him. While the bushfires have gradually receded from public view, because a global pandemic triggering the biggest economic shock since the Great Depression trumps a once-in-a-century climate change–fuelled natural disaster, Morrison's failure during the first crisis shaped how he would respond to the second. Morrison doesn't want to get into what he learnt from the bushfires with me. "I'm not going to go back over that again," he says. But colleagues say the government's pandemic response would likely have been different without the prelude of the bushfire emergency.

Christian Porter says the acquired hypervigilance following the bushfires wasn't just Morrison's. The whole cabinet emerged on edge from the challenges of the summer. Ever the film buff, Porter invokes a thriller to make his point.

> There is a really frightening scene in that film *Deliverance*. They get into trouble with the locals, right? It starts off slowly, it's hard to pick precisely the point at which you really know you are in trouble. This experience has been like that. It's hard to pinpoint exactly when the water for the frog in the pot was getting too hot. Even with retrospect it is impossible to do, but I think we all had an early experience with the bushfires about the wisdom of an over-precautionary and over-preparatory response, so planning for the worst, hoping for the best. I think there was probably a little bit of the cabinet being on edge, which was probably exactly what was needed in all of the circumstances.

People sometimes assume leaders are always playing three-dimensional chess, that it is obvious in the fog of decision-making exactly when various things should happen. Journalists feed these false narratives by playing camel jockey, by upbraiding the political class for not recognising a turning point that is only really visible in hindsight. As Sinodinos notes, politics, fundamentally, is the art of making decisions based on imperfect information. Instinct matters as much as intellect.

When this essay was originally commissioned, it was intended to be a profile of Morrison. Strangely, the man who leads Australia in these complex and difficult times is remarkably unstudied. Morrison is unstudied, in part, because it's hard to get a fix on him. I watch Morrison for a living, but I find him confounding in a number of respects. To borrow from Gertrude Stein, there's no there there. The more you look, the less you see, because his surface is reflective.

He's ubiquitous, like all ambitious politicians. He projects a prime ministerial character – a product, if you will – which presumably is grounded in personal truths. But he's private too. Intimates, at least in political life, are few, and kept close. People say he partitions the three components of his life – politics, family, faith – and there are significant boundaries. If you are a true Morrison *mate*, if you exist durably in the realm beyond the transactions, beyond what the prime minister needs in the political moment, that categorisation has meaning. It's not a term of art, bestowed lightly, as extroverts tend to bestow it, on the last person they met.

People will bristle at the comparison, but the deep reserve at Morrison's core reminds me of Julia Gillard, another prime minister who turned up to battle with a shield and made it her business to get things done. It's an odd comparison, I know, but like Gillard, Morrison is watchful. Years ago, when I was at *The Age* and he was a new federal MP, a couple of colleagues and I went out to dinner with a group of up-and-coming Liberal MPs, including Greg Hunt, who barely drew breath, and Morrison, who only spoke when he wanted to make a point. His vigilance was what I took from that fleeting encounter.

I'd forgotten that quality of his, but then saw it again in the Oval Office, of all places. I was in Washington reporting on Morrison's visit in 2019, and we all endured a mad press conference where Donald Trump floated and then scotched a nuclear strike on Iran in the space of ten minutes. While Trump veered and swerved, Morrison was scanning the room without making a performance of it, logging the various reactions. Morrison can read a room. Not every politician can.

I didn't have much to do with him coming up through the ranks, because his portfolios weren't areas I covered closely. I wasn't useful to him, so I wasn't a person he cultivated. Pre-COVID, Morrison's approach to the media was simple: he or his trusted staff dealt with journalists who got the job done for him. Doing the job is amplifying the line, or flying the required kite, with little or no backchat. Everyone else got short shrift.

Most politicians are transactional both with colleagues and with journalists. This is not a quality singular to Morrison. But some deploy charm or flattery to soften the edges. Morrison has never felt the need to be charming. During the pandemic, his approach with the media evolved, because his needs had changed. With the public hanging on every development, Morrison needed more media outlets to be able to follow his breadcrumbs and decode his statements, so he tweaked his approach. He became more inclusive, more patient and more explanatory. There were regular background briefings for Canberra news bureau chiefs at the height of the crisis, which informed a lot of the contemporaneous reporting. These sessions were extremely helpful: facts and figures, a bit more insight into the direction of the thinking.

The former South Australian crossbench senator Nick Xenophon has a story about Morrison which epitomises the prime minister's transactional tendencies. The two bumped into one another during the strange week in 2016 when the parliament had been prorogued for the federal election, but Turnbull had brought the chambers back to pass the budget, which required a surreal formal opening presided over by the governor-general. Lower house MPs had filed into the Senate chamber for the governor-general's speech, and were in the process of filing out when the milling throng brought Xenophon and Morrison together. Xenophon at that time was an influential player in the Senate, a vote the government needed periodically. "I said to [Morrison] it would be good to catch up for a coffee, because I actually enjoyed talking to him about policy," Xenophon recalls. "He looked at me askance and said, 'What for?' I said just to catch up and have a chat about issues. He said, 'No, mate. I'm purely transactional.'"

Xenophon laughs at the memory, but he wasn't laughing at the time. "It was pretty blunt. It was a pretty terse response, basically fobbing me off. I thought, okay. I felt a bit chastised. I thought this isn't someone you want to shoot the breeze with. 'I'm purely transactional.' I was taken aback. I thought I had worked pretty constructively with him, even on the asylum seeker issue."

There are plenty of stories about Morrison's short shrift, and certainly engaged voters who watch politics regularly will have caught glimpses of it. People will have logged the short fuse, the prime ministerial chin that juts out when he's displeased with a line of questioning. Morrison's leadership of the Liberal Party was born in crisis, and crisis has persisted. You can't hide who you are in a crisis. You can wear a mask, but truth still vents around the edges, like a mist.

Morrison has rusted-on internal supporters, but he isn't well liked in politics. He plays to win, and people who play to win tend to accumulate enemies. In his recent memoir, Turnbull says Morrison displayed only limited interest in policy during their period sharing a cabinet table. This could be a caustic aside, and given their fraught history it may be an unfair characterisation – but it's an observation that other contemporaries are happy to reinforce. Morrison was interested in preventing the legalisation of same-sex marriage, Turnbull says. Colleagues add the maintenance of the school chaplains program to his personal preoccupation list.

John Howard was both pragmatist and ideologue. Like Morrison, Howard appealed to people who felt they weren't represented by the cultural elites – a cohort dubbed variously "the forgotten people" by Robert Menzies, the "silent majority" by Richard Nixon and, most recently, the "quiet Australians," Morrison's contribution to the lexicon. But Howard had a clear political philosophy which manifested in a policy agenda: tax reform, labour-market deregulation and taking on union power, including that high-octane confrontation on the Australian waterfront. John Kunkel, now Morrison's chief of staff, wrote speeches for Howard in the closing years of his prime ministership. In a piece published in 2008,

Kunkel noted that Howard's economic liberalism wasn't pure, "but it was a core part of his political makeup that, ultimately, tested the limits of what the Australian political system would bear." It was clear what Howard's liberalism was. The economic recovery required after COVID will define a Morrison project, events will demand that. But going in, it is difficult to identify Morrison's abiding objectives in public life. What hill would Scott Morrison die on? Howard died on the hill of WorkChoices, losing his seat in the 2007 election. But as Morrison said in 2017, the post-GFC Liberal Party isn't about converting Australians to its orthodoxies and verities: it is about governing from the ground up.

If you govern from the ground up, you are a moving target. You keep yourself several steps ahead of any attempt to categorise you. You are what you need to be. As a thought experiment, I asked one of my colleagues recently to describe Morrison to me in a sentence. "All power and no responsibility," was the sentence; a political leader both present and, when necessary, absent, minus a forwarding address. I'm not sure about "no" responsibility. I'm certain Morrison feels the weight of the decisions that events have forced him to make. But there's some truth to my colleague's shorthand. When adversity strikes, when he loses control of the tempo, when accountability becomes oppressive, the prime minister becomes the man who wasn't there. That's a fixed point in the Scott Morrison story. He doesn't mind being asked questions, being asked to explain – what he minds is answering the questions.

By temperament, Morrison is a power player, not a persuader. Not all prime ministers are comfortable with power when they obtain it. Power and pressure can be paralysing. We saw that with Rudd. Some prime ministers make decisions by not making decisions. But Morrison likes to make decisions. He likes levers. He's happy to pull them if he has them. Some colleagues argue that's what went wrong for the prime minister during the bushfires: Morrison was reduced to being a bystander.

Morrison was distracted at the onset of the fires, and doubtless exhausted at the end of a gruelling political year. Imposing the campaign director mindset on this problem, he clearly didn't see the fires as his project to manage, and he said he had made a promise to his wife and children to take a holiday with them. Presumably Morrison's family thought they would get him back after the election he was supposed to lose in May, but that aspiration was thwarted by the miracle victory. Morrison went to Hawaii, but the office was worried enough about the negative political implications to try to suppress that story being written. How dreadful that holiday must have been.

As well as the cursed holiday becoming, as superficially inconsequential things often do, a potent symbol of a prime minister happy to kick back while the country burnt, Morrison had a more profound problem. He was thwarted by the federation. People wanted national leadership, but he couldn't influence the response. He couldn't order fire trucks onto fire grounds. The premiers were in command. There were no levers to pull. The catastrophe also triggered a community debate about climate change, which is always dangerous for Liberal leaders. Morrison couldn't talk about the root cause of the disaster, climate change, because that's quicksand, and the only chance he has of crafting a medium-term solution on that issue is not to talk about it. That's the price of entry for Liberal leaders. That is Tony Abbott's only durable contribution to public life.

Rendered impotent by the federation, and caught between internal constituencies, Morrison struggled to adopt the crisis as his own cause. It's helpful here to linger around the idea I floated a minute ago, that Morrison is a power politician, not a persuader. In the bushfires, there was, actually, a role for Morrison: leader, listener, unifier, empathiser-in-chief. A persuasion politician would have got that instinctively. A persuasion politician would have understood there was a story arc to narrate and would have set about doing that. But this mode of politics is new territory for Morrison. He'd tried a bit of that style of politics during the drought tours that preceded the bushfires, but it was clear he was still finding his feet. He had a reason to journey about the country empathising: grants to unveil, consultations to do. Busy work. But the idea of hogging a camera during the bushfires just to empathise or lead in an abstract sense isn't really Morrison's bag. He's a doer – not a bard. He wants solutions, not seminars.

The prime minister only began to stabilise the politics of the bushfire emergency when he eventually found something to do. He ordered ADF reservists onto the fire grounds. Curiously enough, the relevant provisions in the *Defence Act* require the governor-general to exercise that power only on the advice of the minister for defence, which necessitated a hasty return of the portfolio minister, Senator Linda Reynolds, from a Bali holiday to sign the relevant instruments. The NSW Rural Fire Service chief Shane Fitzsimmons, who was running operations in the state, didn't hide his irritation with Morrison complicating things at the practical level, but the intervention gave the prime minister a command point, a ledge on a cliff face, a place to regroup before clawing back.

The interesting thing about Morrison, transitioning from one crisis to the next, is how much the prime minister learnt in a short space of time. It's not surprising at one level, because we've already encountered Morrison the watcher. But he's also shown an ability to learn from past cock-ups. Morrison has taken a beating in full public view. He won't ruminate on that beating and its lessons with me. The experience still rankles. But he's been prepared to accept, at least implicitly, that his approach needed improvement. If he felt misrepresented during that period, he is determined that this period will be different.

The bushfires rendered him a bystander. He reacted to that lesson by projecting himself into the centre of the next crisis, COVID-19. The pandemic is still a federated crisis, but Canberra has more levers: biosecurity controls, border enforcement, shared interests in the public and private health systems, and economic policy – and the prime minister pulled every one of them.

As we've outlined, Morrison moved quickly on 13 March to corral the premiers in the National Cabinet structure; to bind the leadership of the country in shared purpose. Not to be rendered surplus to requirements by the federation a second time, he would co-govern with the premiers rather than hang around looking hapless, trying to prompt traumatised people to shake his hand, which remains one of the most powerful images of Morrison's miscues in the fires.

The price of entry for Morrison was being pushed harder on the public health restrictions than he wanted to go initially. He had to cop border closures. He supported efforts by Clive Palmer to try to prise the borders back open, but then had to clamber out of the resistance because of the weight of public opinion in Western Australia, and to preserve his relationship with the WA premier, Mark McGowan. He had to compromise because there was no other choice. Perhaps in the process he was learning the utility of compromise.

As well as governing in coalition with the premiers, Morrison also co-opted elements of civil society that he's historically been at loggerheads with, which not only assisted in the practical management of a crisis and broadened the nature of his political advice, but also turned the volume down. Since the digital disruption, the rise of social media, and the hollowing out of newsrooms, criticism of political leaders in the public arena has become more strident as opinions (cheap) have increasingly substituted for news gathering and dispassionate investigation (expensive). Morrison wanted the crisis to subdue the cacophony, and he largely succeeded in that objective during the first wave. I suspect this lulling exercise will be harder to achieve in the second, because tempers are shorter, people are more anxious and the governing record is tangible. At the beginning, there were no facts to know, and no ideas to contest. Now, there is an accumulation of facts. When there's a record, gravity asserts itself. The inquisitions and the blame-shifting start. It becomes harder to claim that mishaps were someone else's when the chain of evidence is secure, and in the hands of the prosecutor.

Doubtless there were numerous behind-the-scenes interventions that helped drive Morrison's post-bushfires reset. But the fact is, Morrison learnt from the cock-up. The prime minister is not fixed. He is still evolving. This is an important takeout from the pandemic: our prime minister is protean. This guy can be anything he thinks he needs to be.

It's no great insight to say Morrison is a shape-shifter, a populist, a pragmatist, the master of the quick getaway. We knew this before COVID. But what has been interesting through the COVID-19 period so far is that this stubborn, easily triggered, impatient person, Scott Morrison, has tried to be patient. He has, at times, tried to persuade as well as to pull levers. He understands the times require narration as well as action. People watched him learn, and rewarded the effort. There was a steady rebound in his approval ratings over the first six months of 2020.

Safe now in civilian life, Xenophon has a question about the man who cut him dead in 2016. He doesn't know the answer, and neither do I, but it's the right question to ask. "I now wonder whether the coronavirus crisis, which has transfixed and transformed the nation, has changed him too. Has this changed Scott Morrison as well? Has it changed him into someone who is less transactional and more consensus-driven, maybe someone who is willing to have a cup of coffee with someone when there is nothing in it for him?"

Let's consider faith. Faith is very important to the prime minister. Morrison leaves that door ajar to allow viewing from a distance, but the door closes and deadlocks when inquisitors and voyeurs get too close. Australia's prime minister prays. Believing in God is a significant part of who Morrison is in his private domain. Faith is a place of refuge where he can escape the wicked problems, and the cameras, and the legions of advisers. If you are not a believer, this deep respect for a higher power may feel strange and likely suspect. I'm soft lapsed, so praying doesn't seem strange to me. *God is dwelling in my heart*, we used to trill as students at my Catholic primary school in country New South Wales. *He and I are one.*

In my childhood, the nuns counselled us to strive for the gift of faith. Faith wasn't a given. It wasn't an absolute. It was something God bestowed upon people who had the humility to ask for it and the resolve to bend to God's will. Uncertainty was embedded in this process. Faith, in the tradition I was raised in, was always shadowed by doubt. Was it like that for Morrison, growing up in a different religious tradition? When I look at the prime minister, I see certainty, and not a trace of doubt. The prime minister's certainties, practical and professional, are as squat and reinforced as an armoured tank. Certainty fuels the work ethic, the self-belief, and it likely facilitates the compromises and evasions of political life, because if you are certain, if you have banished doubt, then these are actions taken in the service of a larger calling, which in this world is public service.

Morrison projects like a person who feels called to lead, compelled to be the captain-coach of a country in crisis. What's unclear to me is whether the prime minister's religious belief is cultural or doctrinal; I strongly suspect the latter, but this is speculation, not knowledge. I'm a cultural Catholic. My spiritual topography is curved, not rigid; it's grey, and misting, not black and white. But many of the true believers, the non-lapsed, are literalists. Some believe in predestination, salvation and eternal banishment as absolutes. God created the world. Moses parted the sea. Noah saved the animals in the flood. This kind of spirituality is rigid. I'd like to unpick this with him, the fundamentals of his religious belief, given it anchors him. But he won't go there. "Faith is enormously important to me and there are a range of things I do around my faith," he says. "But I don't want to go into those. I'm uneasy. It always becomes an issue if I talk about it. It is such a personal thing, and no matter how I explain it, it will be misinterpreted."

At one point during the crisis, Morrison was captured in devotion during a Zoom prayer group. A fragment of the session later turned up on YouTube. In the clip, Morrison characterises his faith as confidence, encouragement, reassurance. The COVID-19 pandemic, he said, was like the moment Moses looked out at the sea. Moses held up his staff and on they went. It was a moment of great faith. Implicitly in this recounting, Moses exhibited a moment of great leadership. Morrison was clear that he balanced deep faith with expert advice and evidence. He told participants on the call he had to take decisions on the basis of strong advice. "My faith gives me enormous encouragement in how I can make those decisions." Morrison drew on two verses. The first was a psalm. *The righteous cry out and the Lord hears them.* The second was from the prophet Isaiah. "Your people will rebuild the ancient ruins and will raise up the age-old foundations; you will be called repairer of broken walls, restorer of streets with dwellings." Morrison on the Zoom call categorised that verse as "a prophecy over our nation." Likely he meant a prophecy over his own prime ministership: the repairer of broken walls. That combination of practicality and higher purpose, the idea that God rewards faithfulness by providing a purpose for those who serve him, would appeal.

When we meet in July, I ask him about the fragment from Isaiah. "I read that, because I read often, and it resonated," Morrison says. He tells me he found that particular verse during the bushfires. Interesting you found it then, I prompt. "We are rebuilding," he says. There's no further elaboration. I'm on the threshold, but he won't let me cross.

We can proceed in generalities. He tells me faith has been sustenance during the pandemic. Since the third week in January, there has been work, family and faith. That's it. Life pared back to the essentials. "Suffice to say, I pray, and I do a lot of it," he says. "Faith is an important part of my family life. Family is central to sustaining all things. When Jen and the kids came down [to Canberra], that was really important. I could walk out of here and into home and I was with them. It's been harder since they've gone home – a lot harder, because I'm on my own. But having them here during that really difficult time was really good."

Faith was also an inheritance from his father, John. John was a policeman, and, later, in local government. When Morrison looks at you, you feel him sizing up which side of the line you are on. You also feel his aversion if he intuits you are on the wrong side. I wonder if that's Dad's habit – the gaze of an officer who has to make instant evaluations that might save their own life and the lives of others – embedded in the son. I ask Morrison what his father taught him. "My father never ducked his responsibility. He had a keen sense of duty. Whenever something particularly difficult was happening in the broader family, not just within our own family, Dad would always step up and take charge. He was the one everyone would look to. He never waited."

I ask Morrison whether his father made mistakes by not waiting. I've seen Morrison do that. When his energy minister, Angus Taylor, found himself under investigation by NSW police because of a dodgy document he used to attack the lord mayor of Sydney, Clover Moore, Morrison rashly declared he would ring the state police commissioner. He tripped over his own perpetual motion, his own compulsion to be a fixer. I wrote at the time that the country needed a prime minister, not a saviour. "Dad made heaps of mistakes and he would be the first to say so, but the mistake he never made was failing to step up. Dad was someone who was very keen to drum into [brother] Alan and I our responsibilities by his own examples. You knew if you weren't measuring up – he had a way of making sure you knew."

The purpose of touching down on faith is to counterpoise my account of Morrison the protean: a pragmatic populist. He is that, of course, he is absolutely that. But it would be a mistake to conclude that nothing lives at Morrison's core. Believing in God is at the core of this person, this politician, this prime minister, and faith is the thread that links him to many of the people he cares about, both inside and outside politics. Faith is a hinterland, a community, a fellowship of like-minded people. It also links him to many voters. "A lot of people pray for me around the country, thousands, if not millions," he says. "They send me notes. I find that really encouraging." When Morrison secured the leadership of the Liberal Party, some Pentecostal pastors in Australia described his ascension as a miracle of God.

Morrison wants voters to know he believes in God. Periodically, he shows them. He invited the cameras in with him to the Horizon Church in Sutherland on Easter Sunday during the 2019 election campaign. Just before voters went to the polls, he promised voters he would "burn for you every day" if he won the election. I was at the National Press Club when he said this, and the declaration felt intense. In the room, it jarred. But the phrase is invoked in Morrison's religious tradition to signify dedication to a cause. When he won, he told supporters he had always believed in miracles. There's both absolute sincerity and political method in this signalling. Pentecostalism is a relatively small Christian denomination in Australia, but growing rapidly. According to the Census, its ranks grew from around 220,000 in 2006 to 260,500 in 2016, an increase of 18 per cent at a time when the ranks of all Christian denominations declined by 4 per cent.

In Morrison's first speech to parliament, he argued Australia was not a secular country, it was a free country. Leaders like William Wilberforce and Desmond Tutu stood for the immutable truths and principles of the Christian faith, Morrison said.

> They transformed their nations and, indeed, the world in the process … From my faith I derive the values of loving-kindness, justice and righteousness, to act with compassion and kindness,

> acknowledging our common humanity, and to consider the welfare of others; to fight for a fair go for everyone to fulfil their human potential and to remove whatever unjust obstacles stand in their way, including diminishing their personal responsibility for their own wellbeing; and to do what is right, to respect the rule of law, the sanctity of human life and the moral integrity of marriage and the family. We must recognise an unchanging and absolute standard of what is good and what is evil.

So, faith sits at the core of the man. Morrison as Christian prime minister is also part of the package, a wedge on the prime ministerial pie chart, a point of relatability with some voters. He wants that wedge in plain sight, but not over-hyped, and certainly not interrogated. "I'm very careful not to make a show of it," he says.

Many people reading this essay will have their own bespoke pie chart of Morrison: prime ministerial commodity, with customised wedges. Fans of the prime minister will have wedges like statesman, scholar, dynamo. The haters – well, probably best not to go there. Mine looks a bit like this. He's a bloke's bloke. I sometimes wonder how he tests with women, because he can be aggressive in making his point. Many women meet variants of Morrison most days in meetings: the bloke who likes to punch it home. "Go Sharks" and all that represents – the shorthand for suburban Scott – is obviously on the pie chart. So is the nuts-and-bolts political animal, heavy on the party research, light on the Edmund Burke. Devoted family man. I doubt he does the washing, or the grocery shopping without a list, but he's modern enough to cook a curry, or to go to a Tina Arena concert with Jen on date night and have someone pop that up on Instagram. The Morrison plumb line is traditional, implacable. He presents as affable but he's actually intense. He masks the intensity with hail fellow well met, and a light seasoning of Dad jokes.

There needs to be a wedge addressing his political values, but nailing this requires a bit more exploration. We can start with his self-described pandemic philosophy: non-ideological conservatism, and "a-partisanship."

Morrison is looking for a prompt. Sitting across the table is one of his media advisers, Lauren Gianoli, a former television journalist. "What's the name of that group?" Morrison asks her. "GetUp," Lauren volunteers, after a short reflection. "I think they misunderstood conservatives," Morrison says.

Morrison is referring to the positive reaction in progressive circles when the government unveiled the two income-support programs, JobSeeker and JobKeeper. When the government doubled Newstart and signed off on the wage subsidy there was a frisson of "ideological excitement," he says, from progressive activists welcoming a Road to Damascus conversion. But they missed the point. Intervening in that way at that time, he says, wasn't about ideology. "Why did I do JobKeeper and JobSeeker? Because the security of the country was under threat. I wasn't setting up some long-term welfare program."

"The nation's economy was under threat. The nation's social stability was under threat if this wasn't done. You don't do it forever. If you leave the support in too long, it actually harms the economic interest and it changes all the incentives in the labour market. That can cause real long-term damage. Getting it there and getting it back is the challenge, but they saw it as a leftie thing. It wasn't a leftie thing. It was the tool needed to do that job. That's why it was done. There was no ideology behind it at all."

A couple of things here. I reckon universities, and temporary workers, and other groups pushed off the fiscal life raft, would take issue with Morrison's description of policy-making absent ideology. I suspect they would think that ideology may have played a role in who was in and who was out. I also doubt the progressive activists of GetUp saw the programs as "a leftie thing." It's more likely they saw an opportunity to launch a call to action, which is what groups like GetUp do – translate transient opportunities in national affairs into permanent campaigns. "Let's keep Newstart at this expanded rate. Click this button to lobby your local MP. Click here to contribute to the cause."

In any case, Morrison doesn't really care about GetUp in this homily. He's decanting his own philosophy by defining his opponents, which is what political combatants do. Morrison's a partisan, blue team to the core, but his political philosophy is hard to pin down, because it is predominantly trouble-shooting. By instinct, as we have seen, Morrison is a power player and a populist, not a philosopher; a repairer of walls, not a writer of manifestos. If there's consistency to be found, it's this: Morrison looks for opportunity to show voters he's practical. He has some of the tendencies and inclinations of the authoritarian populist, but you wouldn't want to over-egg that either, because he hasn't landed yet. Right now, the dominant quality is brusque managerialism.

Just before the last federal election, my *Guardian* colleague Sarah Martin trawled through Morrison's school yearbooks looking for ancient gems to embed in a profile. The hunt for durable insights delivered. She discovered Morrison was cast as the Artful Dodger in the school musical production of *Oliver!* in 1982 ("I'd Do Anything" being one of the more memorable anthems of the resourceful pickpocket and street urchin). Fifteen-year-old Morrison, captain of his Year 10 rowing four, noted he was known for his "psyche-up sessions and aggravating coaching suggestions." He described himself as "the brains of the crew, plotting the race strategies." This is likely adolescent self-satire, but the accuracy of the report stands.

In 2020, occupying the most powerful position in the country, Morrison is still plotting race strategies, and doing whatever it takes, but he is also still deciding what sort of leader he will be. He's still journeying to the core of his own project. As well as creating a track record of actions that will form the contours of a prime ministership, Morrison is refining his political identity in plain sight. He dials himself up and down, tuning to remove the static. I've seen him try on a Trump suit to see if that fits, and discard it as not quite right (although I suspect that's still in the wardrobe in case he needs it). I've seen him seek to inflame and divide, and I've seen him bring people together.

You see the constant refining with his word pictures. This is a prime minister always on the hunt for a cut-through line or analogy. He's relentless, working through iteration after iteration. Think about the various descriptions of former Labor leader Bill Shorten. He hammered "Unbelieva-Bill" for a bit. During one outing in June 2018, Morrison hurled that same sobriquet nine times, like a projectile at a window. He wants the optimal moment. He's prepared to work to get it. He doesn't lose interest. Eventually, he or the brains trust around him found "the Bill you can't afford." "The Bill Australia can't afford." The sweet spot. The earworm. The precise chord progression that the three-chord pop song needed to make it "Bad Moon Rising" rather than a kid noodling valiantly in his bedroom. Bye-bye, Bill.

Because he is a perpetual-motion machine, if you start from a fixed position, from a set predisposition, you'll always be coming at Morrison the wrong way, because he doesn't start from a set position, apart from the persistent reflex to identify what needs fixing. He tells me politics is about finding the right answer, and to do this you need to suspend your political brain. I ask him to explain what he means by this. It seems highly unlikely to me that a political animal like Morrison ever suspends his political brain, but I'm curious to hear the rationale.

To illustrate, he tracks back to his time in the immigration portfolio. Morrison says before 2013, the idea of turning back boats to Indonesia was not universally popular with Australian voters. He says the public split 50/50 on the question. But Tony Abbott had promised to stop the boats. No ifs, buts or maybes. Stop the boats was the election promise. After assessing the range of options, Morrison's view was that turn-backs would work. That was the practical fix, and the fix was required because "if I don't fix it – well, we are done. You've got to have the right answer, and you can't let the politics stop you from coming up with the right answer, because if you don't get the right answer, you will fail, and the worst thing in politics is failing.

"I'm a problem-solver. They say good policy is good politics – well, actually, good problem-solving is even better. That's what I mean by suspending ideology – you've got to find the right answer."

Morrison isn't enamoured of the conventions of politics. Parliament clearly annoys him. He disdains procedures others hold to be sacred. Despite being naturally combative, he doesn't crave the theatre of the bear-pit, like a Keating or a Howard. While I accept the point Sinodinos made to me about Morrison liking all aspects of the job, he's not enamoured with that element of the life, that ritualised coming together of competing philosophies. The institution constrains him, it imposes routines and rituals, and Morrison is always packed for flight.

He's also irritated by the frequent characterisation of National Cabinet as a bipartisan exercise, as an enlightened synthesis of competing world-views. Again, in his estimation, this is the wrong starting point for analysis. "This whole idea that things need to be bipartisan – I don't understand this," Morrison says.

> It's not what we were doing. It wasn't bipartisanship in the National Cabinet, it was government, and government is a practical exercise.
>
> The people who needed to be in the room were not people who needed to represent different political ideologies and philosophies. It needed to be people in the room who were responsible for people's health and safety and could make decisions and apply resources. If you couldn't do that, there was no place for you at the table.
>
> Bipartisanship – I don't know what that means. A-partisanship, well that matters, coming together in the national interest. If you've got something to add to that cause, well, you are welcome. The idea that bipartisanship is some goal in itself, I don't get that.

I ask whether he thinks the pandemic will kill activism, because Australians will be more focused on their health and their material well-being – and whether the crisis has suspended ideology. He claims not to have considered the chilling effect of the crisis on activism, which is possible given the volume of pandemic-related deliberations, but, I think, unlikely given the way his political brain works. Morrison was so irritated by activism at the end of last year, at least the kind of activism that the Coalition and the resources industry finds inconvenient, that he branded climate protesters "anarchists" and foreshadowed a crackdown on various forms of protests during a speech claiming progressives were trying to cancel the liberty of the quiet Australians. Activism made his life hell during the bushfires. This prime minister thinks about activism, and how it might shift the centre of Australian politics.

I'm interested in how Morrison thinks his pragmatism sits with more ideological colleagues. The key test of this will be how quickly the government seeks to unwind the fiscal support it deployed during the crisis. We got the first litmus test of this in July, when Morrison extended but cut the JobSeeker and JobKeeper payments; a sense of hastening slowly towards an exit. But cutting the payments was risky, given all the variables, and the government was forced to amend its own exit strategy only a couple of weeks later, when events in Victoria demanded a longer tail of income support. Morrison was back to whatever it takes without skipping a beat. I ask Morrison whether he accepts that stimulus will be needed for quite a long period of time, given that the prospect of a V-shaped recovery looks increasingly remote. On current indications, Australia is heading for a recession that will be worse than those of the early 1980s and early 1990s. The Reserve Bank and the IMF are clear that economies will need substantial support. But stimulus isn't a word small-government people like. Stimulus is not a banned word, but it's not a welcome one either.

Which is why Morrison doesn't use it. "I don't know if I'd describe it as stimulus. It can be described as stimulus, but that's probably not how I think of it. There's an aggregate demand policy which will be important because the COVID economy is still constrained by definition. International borders are closed and social distancing restraints will artificially limit the size of your economy. That will have implications for aggregate demand, so there is an obvious gap there." An aggregate demand policy is stimulus, isn't it? "It is supporting aggregate demand," he says, before changing the subject. As well he might, given that the concept of aggregate demand is fundamental to Keynesian analysis. The need for government spending to support demand and bring the economy out of protracted slumps was the main policy prescription advanced by John Maynard Keynes.

Morrison's caution here is illustrative. I ask him how long the ideologues in the government will tolerate the government's shape-shift. The pandemic has been stressful and all-consuming, and it's entirely possible the worst is yet to come. But it has also given Morrison the operating conditions he prefers: a suspension of conventions he has little respect for, and lots of latitude. Morrison is still determining what sort of prime minister he will be, but doing that is about more than sating your own desires. It requires a judgment about what your colleagues will tolerate. Success creates the opportunity for prolonged self-expression; adversity makes a political leader a creature of the firm. As a player in the removal of Tony Abbott and a beneficiary of the demise of Malcolm Turnbull, Morrison knows this all too well.

Asked about his freedom to move, he says: "A crisis brings its own sort of focus, and its own tolerance for leaders to just get on with things."

How long does the tolerance stretch for, then? There's the hint of a smile at the other end of the table.

"We'll find out," Morrison says. "We'll find out. We are still in the crisis, though, and we can't be complacent about it."

A GLOBAL CHALLENGE, MINUS A GLOBAL SOLUTION

This crisis has been a mirror. It has reflected the underlying truths of nations.

In America, the reflection has been dystopian, the horrors captured elegiacally by gifted writers such as David Remnick and George Packer. In Britain, the experience has been chaotic. First, the strategy was herd immunity. Then, suddenly, it wasn't. Then Boris Johnson found himself in intensive care. Health systems in Spain and Italy couldn't cope with a disaster that their governments had failed to manage. Europe was devastated, with Germany, led by the serially stoic Angela Merkel, the honourable exception. In China, the experience has been Orwellian. The regime initially punished doctors trying to warn of the impending crisis in Wuhan, then locked down populations with brutal efficiency, then tried to muddy the waters about the origins of a pandemic, then attempted to reposition as altruistic handmaidens to Italy and other countries battling the outbreak – the model managers of the pandemic with valuable wisdom to export. Fearing both damage to its international standing and the potential for political unrest at home, the Chinese government has engaged in active disinformation campaigns about the origins of the pandemic. A foreign ministry spokesman, Lijian Zhao, has shared material on social platforms contending America, not Wuhan, is responsible for COVID-19.

The pandemic is a global problem that has failed to trigger a coordinated global response. It has exposed the underlying weakness of global institutions. It demonstrated that America has withdrawn from the moral responsibility of global leadership. America, as George Packer noted in a funereal essay in *The Atlantic*, couldn't even save itself. It was revealed to be "a beggar nation in utter chaos." During the month of March – the critical month where Australian political leaders worked to stabilise the crisis – "Americans woke up to find themselves citizens of a failed state, with no national plan – no coherent instructions at all."

The crisis has also inflamed geopolitical tensions between the major powers, as the Trump administration sought to inoculate itself against its own maladministration by ramping up nativist rhetoric about the "Chinese virus," and Beijing sought to capitalise on the vacuum in American leadership – a dangerous dance that will continue through the second half of 2020, as the Chinese president seeks to assert domestic control over his population and Trump drags an exhausted and angry world behind his deranged but mesmerising march to the polls in November.

Richard Haass, the president of the Council on Foreign Relations, says this crisis hasn't changed the direction of world history so much as accelerated it. We already inhabit a post-American world. There was already fatigue with globalisation, and great-power competition imperiling global stability and prosperity. There was already rising nationalism, and visceral political resistance in many countries to integration and the free movement of people. "Waning American leadership, faltering global cooperation, great-power discord: all of these characterized the international environment before the appearance of COVID-19, and the pandemic has brought them into sharper-than-ever relief," Haass says. "They are likely to be even more prominent features of the world that follows." We'd arrived there before COVID, but the pandemic has made it plain that we now inhabit the era of the nation. When the threat arrived, nations with varying speed and efficiency rolled down the shutters and formulated their own responses. In federations like Australia and America, many of the interventions, Haass notes, have been sub-national. They've been led by state, provincial and local governments.

While American intellectuals mourn their failure of political leadership, and the Republic buries the human sacrifices of its institutional failure, the comparative competence of the Australian response, at least during the first wave, seems to have stirred domestic sentiments of Australian exceptionalism. The pandemic has also triggered a debate about the need to boost the sovereign capability of the nation-state, both here and elsewhere. This conversation began at the onset of the pandemic, when global supply chains were profoundly disrupted because of China's dominance in manufacturing. Business and think-tank voices were quick out of the blocks declaring Australia needed to bring manufacturing back onshore.

Some previous Liberal governments would have been hostile to a new form of protectionism festooned in a cloak of enlightened nationalism, and to the idea of governments picking winners, but the Liberal Party of the current era has a very high tolerance for government intervention. In defence, the Coalition runs a $200-billion procurement program on a sovereign capability rationale. In energy policy, the Liberal Party since 2009 has eschewed market mechanisms, including carbon pricing, in favour of clunky state planning, such as underwriting investments in the power grid. At the moment, Liberals are enamoured with a gas-led recovery, a mantra with all the hallmarks of a boondoggle.

I said before that Morrison's conservatism is extreme pragmatism in defence of what he regards as the core of the nation. Morrison throughout his prime ministership, and before it, has been experimenting with language to articulate his own version of nationalism. When the prime minister visited the United States in 2019, Donald Trump told the United Nations the future belonged to patriots, not globalists. Globalism, Trump contended, rallying his base as he was drawn into impeachment, had "exerted a religious pull over past leaders, causing them to ignore their own national interests."

Australia, an open, trading nation, is a beneficiary of the globalised economy, so Morrison, a rational political actor, isn't an isolationist, like Trump. But he understands the vulnerabilities of his era. We live in an age when authoritarians are on the march, and when liberal democracy is under threat. Given that credible research indicates people under thirty aren't sure anymore that democracy is the most preferable form of government, leaders in democratic societies have a problem. Governments have to demonstrate their worth to citizens fundamentally disillusioned with politics-as-usual. That basic insight was at the root of the speech Morrison gave at the Liberal Party's federal council in 2017: politics can't be top-down anymore.

Governing was now about convincing Australians you were "on their side." Rolling forward to the current crisis, "there's been a demonstration of governments solving practical problems and working together," Morrison says. "You can achieve quite a bit, and that improved people's confidence."

This government's record of keeping faith with the public is besmirched by the convulsive leadership intrigues of its three terms, its complete failure to take anything approximating serious action on climate change, its blithe tolerance for the grasping culture of sports rorts, and the obvious heel-dragging on a national integrity commission, to give but a few examples. A generous scorecard would say the record is chequered. But Morrison does grasp the risks: liberal democracy is imperiled when citizens lose respect for institutions.

There's also an obvious political dividend in play. There is a rich political seam to mine if you can somehow find your line and length on 21st-century Australian exceptionalism; if you can both define what it is and present yourself as the custodian and champion of its verities. Australian exceptionalism gives a political leader some architecture onto which shared values can be projected at a time when shared values have been replaced by a relentless coarsening of the culture: polarisation, disinformation, tribalism, contest and crisis.

A populist, and a project manager with the strategic brain of a campaign director, understands that, and will be on a relentless quest for a patriotism that doesn't feel like a retrofit brought to you by Scotty from marketing. A pantomime of patriotism doesn't work in Australia – as Abbott discovered when he festooned his press conferences with flags, ruminated about the threat of death cults, and fantasised about shirtfronting Vladimir Putin. John Howard was much more successful in projecting a rally-round-the-flag nationalism that was forceful, and potent domestically, but a distance short of hysterical. Morrison will want to cultivate his own tone rather than present as an echo of Howard, but the Howard of "we decide who comes here and the circumstances in which they come" will be a working model for what's possible.

So Morrison is on the hunt for a patriotism that can speak its name but doesn't feel contrived. At the root of this is Morrison's increasingly obvious ambition to present to voters as a Cold War leader, so long as the Cold War remains a parable that proceeds on Australia's terms, and so long as tensions don't spiral into unmanageable territory. Narrating the Australia–China relationship is an important piece of the puzzle. Relations with Beijing, fraught before the crisis, have soured during the pandemic. Increasingly, Beijing is starring in a morality play in Australia, cast as the hegemonic villain threatening Australian sovereignty. It is easy to cast China in that role, because the assertive authoritarians in Beijing are using disinformation and interference operations to make China's presence felt, to assert itself as the century's rising power. But the considered hawkishness from the government also mines a shift in the national mood. In 2020, only a quarter of Australians trust China to act responsibly in the world, compared with 52 per cent in 2018.

Australia has always declared it does not have to choose between our most important security ally, America, and our number one trading partner, China. Successive governments have asserted Australia's right to tend both relationships on our own terms. But increasingly it looks like Australia has made a choice. This is complicated, though, and nuanced. While relations have soured with Beijing, and Australia is deeply embedded in the security relationship with the US, Morrison is still trying to preserve Australia's foreign policy independence rather than be dragged into a great-power dogfight. He has been careful not to be co-opted into Trump's trolling of Beijing for domestic political purposes. He sidestepped a Trump-engineered diplomatic imbroglio about the Wuhan lab theory. He's said no – at least so far – to Washington's persistent desire that we conduct freedom-of-navigation exercises close to disputed features in the South China Sea.

In parsing Morrison's efforts to assert his own brand of nationalism, one of the reference texts has to be his late-2019 Lowy speech. About a month after Trump's rhetorical posturing at the UN, Morrison gave a significant speech to the Lowy Institute, a foreign policy think-tank. Freedom,

Morrison said, "depends on our dedication to national sovereignty, the resilience of our institutions, and our protections from foreign interference." Isolationism and protectionism were not in the national interest. Australia must always seek to act responsibly on global issues, engaging in what he called "positive and practical globalism." But Morrison said it did not serve the national interest "when international institutions demand conformity rather than independent cooperation on global issues." This, he said, was negative globalism. Negative globalism happened when "pragmatic international engagement, based on the cooperation of sovereign nation-states, [was] challenged by a new variant of globalism that seeks to elevate global institutions above the authority of nation-states to direct national policies."

Morrison was inventing a world that didn't exist. The power of international agencies to critique Australian action is a function of various covenants that we, a sovereign nation, had signed voluntarily – the protection of refugees, commitments to reduce our greenhouse gas emissions. No direction happens. But the storytelling was about projecting himself as a leader who could bring powerful forces back into alignment, who could achieve a better synthesis between the aspirations of a rational middle power and the irrational and unpredictable forces beyond our borders. The Lowy speech is a fable, where the moral of the story is that nations can still assert control if they have the right leaders.

If resurgent nationalism was a rich political seam to mine pre-COVID, the pandemic has only increased its value. When Morrison introduced the legislation giving effect to JobKeeper at a special sitting of the parliament, the prime minister was again twiddling the sovereignty dials trying to find a static-free frequency. Assuming the grave tone of a radio address during wartime, he told the parliament the nation was currently "under threat" and the government was acting "to protect Australia's sovereignty." When lives and livelihoods were "under attack, our nation's sovereignty is put at risk." Australia, Morrison insisted, was "not a coerced society." We would not "surrender" our sovereignty, which was measured "in our capacity and freedom to live our lives as we choose in a free, open and democratic society" with "a vibrant market economy that underpins our standard of living." Australians would rally to our own cause. How Morrison actualises this rallying to our own cause will define not only his own prime ministership, but also the new centre of gravity for centre-right politics in this country.

Simon Birmingham, the trade minister, strikes a note of caution about the sovereign capability debate and about the risks of resurgent nativism to Australian prosperity. He says it will be necessary for Australia to stocktake national essential capability. "But Australia can't afford for nationalistic sentiment around the world to lead to a wave of global protectionism," he says. "That impedes the ability of our farmers and other exporters to get their goods to market in the future. Our wealth depends on us being an exporting nation." Birmingham says he is working with global counterparts "to make sure we maintain a sensible approach internationally, that we find that sweet spot between the desire that all nations will have to learn lessons out of this, but not to allow those lessons to be misinterpreted as a result of nationalistic or protectionist sentiment."

Given the scale of the disruption the world is facing, and its unknown endpoint, Birmingham's aspiration to remain calm and resist a massive overcorrection is laudable. But the problem is obvious: preserving rationality and enlightened self-interest will require global cooperation. Seeing off resurgent protectionism is not a fight Australia can win on its own. It will require buy-in from like-minded rational actors. This underscores an unavoidable dilemma: the nation may be back in vogue, in part because the quality of global governance has not kept pace with the challenges and disruptions of a globalised world. But many of our most important problems remain global and will require enlightened cooperation to fix.

Australia can't fix free trade if the major powers are intent on reviving protectionism. Europe can't reduce the risks of global warming in the absence of China and America. Perhaps that's why the government squared its own circle. While Morrison shook his fist against negative globalism in the period when he was trying on a Trump suit, the foreign minister, Marise Payne, a calm if muted presence in national affairs – a politician who values that most unfashionable of commodities, strategic silence and personal restraint – tracked us back to multilateralism about six months later.

Payne observed in June that Australia's interests would not be served by retreating from global bodies and "leaving others to shape the global order for us." While calling for reform to ensure UN bodies are "fit for purpose" and "free from undue influence," Payne signalled that Australia would pursue "effective multilateralism." The strategy is threefold. As well as protecting one's own sovereignty and invoking the nation-state as the bedrock of shared values, rational national actors need to shape a new cooperative world order that has some prospect of managing the existential challenges the world faces.

Birmingham talks optimistically about the rise of middle powers. Michael Fullilove, executive director of the Lowy Institute, notes the performance of the superpowers during the COVID crisis has been singularly unimpressive, "but smaller, more agile countries, with rational politicians and effective bureaucracies, have done better." He says, "Middle powers such as Australia have an interest in supporting international health, security and prosperity, and have capability to do so. Perhaps in the future we will see more coalitions of the competent."

I want to persist a little longer with the mirror. What happened here during the opening months of the pandemic? What have we learnt about ourselves?

There has been great tumult. We know that 780,000 Australians lost their jobs in the opening weeks of the first lockdown, and by July more than one million people were out of work. Between mid-March and mid-April – which was the peak of the first wave – more than a million Medicare-funded mental health services were provided by psychologists, psychiatrists and GPs, according to government statistics. There was an 11 per cent increase in contacts to the 1800RESPECT line year-on-year, and an 18 per cent increase in calls to MensLine Australia from people expressing concerns about COVID-19. 1800RESPECT is the national sexual assault and domestic violence counselling and information referral service. MensLine specialises in family and relationship concerns. As the second wave hit Victoria, there was an increase in self-harm–related presentations to hospital, particularly among young people. According to a report in *The Age* in August, there was a 23.3 per cent increase in people presenting at hospitals with a mental illness, and a 29 per cent increase in phone counselling by support services.

How we first responded to the threat paints a picture. At the beginning of COVID, ordinary people acted as though they did not trust the competence of our systems. A cohort of Australians became doomsday preppers, hoarding toilet paper initially, then food and alcohol for the first couple of months of the crisis. Perhaps the hoarders were ahead of the curve. Perhaps they watched the hard lockdowns happening elsewhere, assumed they would also happen here and took rational precautions. Perhaps some of the early movers were entrepreneurial types, developing side hustles selling necessities at inflated prices on the maxim – perhaps it's a cliché – of never wasting a good crisis. The Commonwealth Bank compared credit-card spending in the week ending 20 March 2020 with spending in the same week a year earlier, and found food purchases in supermarkets were up 74 per cent and alcohol sales from bottle shops up nearly 37 per cent. Australian Bureau of Statistics retail sales data for March indicated that sales of canned food, basic medicines and cleaning products spiked 50 per cent in the month.

If we weren't sacked or stood down, and if we weren't health workers, cleaners or supermarket workers, many of our employers sent us home to work. Kids experienced periods of remote education, creating stress for working parents. We all learnt how to upload a background on Zoom so we didn't have to shut the wardrobe door in the bedroom. I worked at home to produce the first draft of this essay. While lockdowns are obviously a living hell for extroverts, triggering frustration and alienation – and while I absolutely respect that the second lockdown in Victoria was much harder to endure than the first – I was sanguine. My work environment is constant clamour. It was peaceful to move out of the relentless bustle of my Parliament House office, and I loved being able to pad around in my socks and have a cup of tea with my husband in the kitchen, or check in with my seventeen-year-old, who had had his final year of schooling profoundly disrupted.

I haven't lost my job so far, although my industry is under terrible pressure. Ken Doctor, an American media analyst, says the impact of the pandemic on advertising has been worse than the hit inflicted by the GFC. He told *BuzzFeed* that for some news organisations, COVID would be an "extinction event." I've lived with insecure employment for a long time now, so my personal objectives are always reasonably modest, but they have become simpler. I want to get to the end of this year with my loved ones safe, and with me still employed.

The most fascinating thing for me in the period of remote work during the first wave was watching my suburb come to life. Normally the streets are pin-drop quiet during daylight hours, because everyone is in an office. But when schools were shut, kids roamed the streets with their siblings, looking for adventures in the neighbouring bush. Fathers and sons passed my window on the way to the local shops, deep in conversation. Because public health imperatives forced social isolation, I found people had a powerful need to connect. Neighbours stood on the opposite sides of driveways to chat at a safe distance. People out on their constitutionals made a study of saying hello to the people they passed, rather than just powering past without making eye contact. Once we'd found our level after the dreadful anxiety of the first few weeks, after we'd adjusted to the shuttered businesses, and roads without commuter traffic, and the constant fear of catching the virus or infecting someone more vulnerable, my community found a new normal. My neighbourhood began to feel like the neighbourhood of my childhood in the 1970s and 1980s. It was a throwback to the pre-productivity economy, before Bob Hawke and Paul Keating and John Howard insisted Australia unfurl itself to the world.

I don't know whether I'm being sentimental in recounting these things. But I feel a powerful need to remember them, to record what I witnessed, to find meaning in fragments of memory and shared experience. Perhaps I need to record these things because sentiment is a protective reflex that insulates people from horror. It's possible, though, that some of us, me included, experienced an interregnum that was both terrifying and a salve of sorts, embarking on a temporary psychic retreat to times before we were on the clock 24/7, before our smartphones enslaved us.

For a period of time I didn't consume, or go out to brunch, or sit in a cinema to try to settle my racing mind. I conceived of myself as something other than a willing conscript to a ceaseless cause called the news cycle. I felt a neighbourhood and a community that I'd never directly participated in because of my punishing work hours brimming and bonding and occasionally roiling around me. I waved at one of my neighbours when he passed my house a couple of times a day walking his dog – a person I'd never waved at despite living three doors up from him for sixteen years. I'm not grateful for this pandemic. I want it to end. I want to remember what it is like not to feel trepidation about the future. But that act of suburban connection felt like a revolution or a redemption, I'm not sure which.

I'm conscious that my experience of the first wave was privileged. This can be my opening experience of COVID-19 because I'm not one of the forgotten people, the people left outside the Commonwealth's fiscal envelope – a refugee, a worker on a temporary visa who has contributed much to Australian society only to be spurned during a crisis. I'm not an artist like my daughter, marooned without steady income from her chosen profession, or a vice-chancellor wondering how their campus functions without the income furnished by thousands of foreign students.

I'm a homebody who was told to go home for a period of time. I'm not an Australian of Asian descent who found themselves racially abused or physically threatened. Nobody spat at me, kicked me or sprayed graffiti on my house. I have not been beaten in my home. I have not been cyberstalked or abused online – at least no more than usual. I have not yet cried with anxiety about what will become of my life savings or my staff. I have not taken my own life because I've lost every cent I poured into my small business, or because social isolation triggered a terrible spiral of despair. I have not had to line up outside Centrelink. I've had wild and restless dreams, particularly at the beginning, but I have not developed clinical anxiety.

I don't live alone. I am not elderly, and desperately lonely without visitors in a nursing home, or terrified about contracting the illness in an aged-care system too deficient to defend my wellbeing. I have not had the experience of being sick, and having to weigh up whether I will pretend I'm not and continue to work in my insecure job because my family needs to eat. I've not been infected with COVID, I'm not in intensive care hovering between life and death. I am as calm as it is possible to be, but, like everyone, I have my moments. Months back, on an evening walk, I discovered the ACT government was building a temporary field hospital for COVID-19 patients on my neighbourhood oval. Overnight, the playing fields that had been the home of boot camps, dog walkers and community cricket and soccer games had been fenced off and had become a construction site. That was a jolt. That felt real, and close.

Profound things have happened to us all in the past few months. One of the most profound is that we seem to want to trust governments and institutions again. Before the winter set in and the second wave loomed, Australians were daring to hope. You could see this renaissance of hope in the data. In the Essential poll that we publish at *Guardian Australia*, voters reconnected, week by week, with the nine governments charged with managing the crisis. In late March, a significant chunk of Australians, particularly people under thirty-four, thought coronavirus was a beat-up. It was the flu – or, as the kids called it, the "boomer remover." Events moved quickly, and perceptions shifted. As the premiers drove the health response, and as Morrison pumped out the largest economic stimulus ever crafted in Canberra, sentiment changed. In the survey published on 24 March, only half the sample (56 per cent) trusted the government to give them reliable information about the pandemic. By 7 April, that was up to 63 per cent. There was another positive performance assessment. On 31 March, 63 per cent of the sample reported feeling informed about the crisis. A week later, that had increased to 70 per cent. While the standing of leaders in Victoria and New South Wales took a hit during the second wave, by August 66 per cent of people in the sample were still trusting governments to provide reliable information.

Daring to trust governments again is a palpable shift, because all the movement in recent times has been in the other direction. Peter Lewis, the executive director of Essential Media, says the survey first detected a decline in institutional trust in the early 2010s, as climate change became weaponised in the Australian system, and "it deteriorated as parties dumped leaders, and tapped the global anti-establishment sentiment that led to Brexit and put Donald Trump into the White House." The tipping point for trust, here and elsewhere, was the global financial crisis – the last significant global shock that revealed the essence of societies to themselves. But in late April 2020, parliaments at a national, state and local level experienced double-digit increases in trust year on year. Trust in political parties was up 11 per cent. It was the same story for business groups and trade unions.

Other social researchers tell me the scale of the COVID-19 crisis has prompted people in Australia to re-evaluate; as one puts it, to develop more reasonable expectations about what governments can do. One researcher I trust says that shift didn't happen during the bushfires. The bushfires triggered a wave of anger and activism. But the pandemic has prompted different responses. As my informant puts it, "there's been a sober view of what's important" – pride in country, reconnection with community, concern about health and economic wellbeing. Events have forced millennials, a socially conscious, post-material generation, to worry about their economic security.

But can this rebound in trust persist in times when no one can predict the future? How durable, how resilient, is the collective desire for rapprochement with institutions? There was a trust rebound in the first six months of 2020 because of perceptions governments were acting competently. The runs were on the board. If the virus crashes through the strategies and structures governments have created to flatten the curve, or if governments are found to have fumbled the health or economic response at critical moments, or if they seek to shirk responsibility for their missteps, if they lie, or obfuscate, or seek to blame others, I suspect the community response to that will be swift and brutal. I fear the renaissance of hope in Australia could be brittle.

Perhaps I imagined it – this pandemic can mess with perception – but I reckon there was a hiatus in tribalism in Australia during the opening weeks of the crisis, a brief armistice. Perhaps this never happened, it is possible it is wishful whimsy on my part, but if it did, that's now in the rear-view mirror. Partisanship and acrimony, division and rancour, is stirring once again, both in politics and the surrounding ecosystems, the mainstream media and social media. The pull of politics-as-usual is visible. We are back in zero-sum conversations. For the disciples of small government, social distancing is an affront to individual liberty, a grave offence against capitalism. Before the pandemic, the bothersome science for this sect was climate change. A pandemic furnished a new echo chamber for relentless, self-serving quackery about the creep of progressive dictatorship, with Daniel Andrews cast in the lead role. Provocation invites a reaction. Politically engaged bystanders weary of monotonous diatribes from the usual suspects, and the #IStandWithDan partisans – an online insurgency intent on policing the discourse – hurl their own rage back into the void of Facebook and Twitter, trying to counter News Corp's latest leaden campaign against the latest progressive leader now considered surplus to requirements. No minds get changed, but the volume increases.

Morrison has struggled to support Andrews during the second wave beyond money and lip-service, and the prime minister also sought to deflect the obvious questions his government has to answer about the lack of rapid response to the COVID-19 onslaught in aged care. The Commonwealth was castigated by the counsel assisting the aged-care royal commission for failing to develop a COVID-19 plan for the sector – a charge the government rejects. But aged care is a federal responsibility, and serious questions remain about whether enough was done to safeguard one of the most vulnerable sectors of society. Andrews has significant questions to answer too. But he's pushed back an inquiry into what went wrong with the management of hotel quarantine: a final report is now not due until November.

The two leaders have positioned for a serious confrontation but stepped back from the brink, perhaps out of uncertainty about who wins a death match. The coming weeks and months will test the resolve of the federation to stick together through this crisis. Will governments prove worthy of renewed trust, or will they squander the opportunity to negotiate a new social licence with Australians?

When this health crisis eventually passes, a new anxiety will replace the fear of COVID-19. Let's call that anxiety: what comes next? As the anthropologist Wade Davis noted recently in a powerful eulogy for the American century in *Rolling Stone*, "pandemics and plagues have a way of shifting the course of history, and not always in a manner immediately evident to the survivors." Australia is not America. Our citizens have been spared the indecency of battling to stay well in a society organised around the mass delusion that radical inequality, and government indifference to the fate of the individual, is the price that must be paid for the prosperity that is always said to trickle down, and never does. Australia is a country where social capital still matters. Social capital is the lever Morrison pulled in March, without much equivocation and without apology, and that saved lives and livelihoods.

But the pandemic has exposed vulnerabilities here as it has everywhere: insecure work, the terrible indignity of ageing, high levels of youth unemployment, the fragility of a world-class university sector, to name but a few – and it is not clear the political class has either the imagination or the clarity to emerge from this trauma with the single-minded ambition of building a better future. Morrison says the COVID-19 recovery will have to be led by the private sector, which is the prelude to a national deregulation agenda that is still taking shape. Perhaps this policy foray will be interesting. It is possible it will yield evidence of original thinking. But there is also a risk it will be little more than a reheating of old ideas. If Morrison's roadmap after the crisis involves reverting to the economic thinking that preceded the global financial crisis, and locking in fossil fuels for another two decades, then Australia is in trouble.

I have documented a crisis and a response. I have tried to record history, and dive beneath those facts and timelines in search of interpretation and meaning. The opening of this pandemic was overwhelming, terrifying, difficult, but the fact is the toughest period is still ahead of us. We are looking at more infections, more deaths, more tragedy, more lost livelihoods. A local recession and a global one, potentially the deepest economic slump since the Great Depression. Recessions are destroyers of dignity, hope and opportunity.

As this essay goes to print, Australia is grappling with the scale of this continuing threat, to both lives and livelihoods. The rate of new infections seems to be trending down, but Victoria remains shuttered and Sydney is on high alert. Defence personnel are standing sentry on the border with New South Wales. Australians have been stoic, because success seemed within our grasp. Can we go on being stoic when anxiety and uncertainty has no end date? Do we have the collective fortitude to live in uncertainty without turning on each other, without hunting scapegoats?

This question applies equally to our political leaders. Will they have the collective fortitude to keep working together if there are incentives to turn on one another? What of Scott Morrison? He has learnt on the job. Will he go on learning? Does he have the capacity to hold a country together through a crisis on this scale? Will his guiding light be the pragmatism that has been largely on show during the pandemic – a spirit of building and fortifying in the national interest – or will he revert to old, tribal habits if the level of adversity deepens? We need him to stay the course on uniting a country. We need the best of him – we need him to be a prime minister who rose to the occasion. But politics remains a deeply toxic business, and duress sometimes brings out the worst in people.

It seems rash to forecast what will be on the other side of this crisis, given we are not out of it, but I sought a couple of submissions. Christian Porter gives a broad prediction. "I think so many things in Australia will change irreversibly on the other side of this," he says. "I've got a four- and a two-year-old. They will grow up in post-corona Australia, they won't know what pre-corona Australia was like. That will be the way we work; we learn; how, when and why we travel; how we eat. Certainly there will be any number of changes to governance and policy and the federation."

He thinks it is possible to use the relationships he has formed during this crisis to reset the industrial relations debate.

> In the IR portfolio, there is a bit of time for fresh beginnings and renewed effort to find common ground. There will clearly be things that remain impossible areas to reach consensus and agreement on, but I think there is an ability to find some more common ground.
>
> I think there are things that clearly need improvement in the IR system from the perspective of having a more productive, vital and competitive economy. Sally [McManus], I'm sure, would say

> there are things that need improvement in the IR system to protect and enhance workers. I think the way forward is to work out where the trades are. It's been a lot of one-way traffic – one side gets in and does what they want, the other side gets in and does what they want. But [we will be] trying to find some kind of ability to trade.

I ask Craig Laundy whether the family business will survive the COVID shock. "At a personal level, we are blessed. We are a four-generation family business. We have a lazy balance sheet and decent cash reserves to get us through. I'm not worried about us. I'm worried about people who fall through the cracks. Not a heap of businesses are in our situation."

I ask Jodie McVernon from the Doherty Institute to tell me what the exit strategy is.

> It's a pathway. This is where all the sensible discussion is happening. It's the idea that society has to live very differently for a very long time. Long-term behavioural change is needed to address risk. Obviously there is a corresponding rush for effective medical therapies. If we can reduce severe outcomes and death, COVID-19 becomes more manageable.
>
> That happened for HIV. I remember going to the AIDS wards in Fairfield Hospital when this was a new disease. It was terrifying. Young men with dementia. People with fungal growths in their heads. Awful. Terrifying. And now that is a lifestyle disease, so we do see effective therapies for terrifying diseases, and if we reduce the risk of severe outcome and death, we do a lot to balance the scales. We would not have to have the same extreme fear of it, but these therapies would need to be available in sufficient quantities for people who need them and we would not want to risk an uncontrolled epidemic. The rate of new cases would overwhelm the capacity of health systems to serve them.

She says Australia, the world, is on a life raft, trying to ride out a monumental tide. Riding out the tide isn't an exercise in perfection, it's an exercise in making the least-worst choices. "I read a piece in *The New York Times* about Wuhan about just how traumatised people are there," McVernon says. "The lockdown has been lifted, but what it was to live through that first wave. We have been spared that. Long-term, that is beneficial for our society; short-term, it is potentially risky because we could think this is all over."

McVernon "thinks" politicians understand the realities, the risks associated with trying to manage a pandemic when there is no vaccine and no guarantee there will ever be one. "Everyone watches the news. Everyone knows there are no easy ways out. The political dilemmas about how to guide societies and economies through this: these are enormous challenges. There are more things to weigh up than just the health impacts. The social measures we are taking also have health impacts.

"The dilemmas are very real. There are no guarantees. There is no certainty."

19 August 2020

SOURCES

Interviews were conducted with Peter Burn in March with Daniel Andrews, Andrew Barr, Simon Birmingham, Josh Frydenberg, Bob Gregory, Craig Laundy, Sally McManus, Jodie McVernon, Brendan Murphy, Martin Parkinson, Christian Porter and Nick Xenophon in April 2020 and again in June 2020; and with Scott Morrison in July 2020. A number of officials and government MPs spoke on background.

8 "*No worst, there is none*": Gerard Manley Hopkins, *Poems and Prose*, Penguin Classics, 1985.

9–10 According to that brief: National Incident Room SitRep, media release and transcript, 21 January 2020, www.health.gov.au/sites/default/files/documents/2020/02/foi-request-1507-correspondence-between-minister-hunt-and-dr-brendan-murphy-email-novel-coronavirus-documents-for-interviews_0.pdf, accessed 6 August 2020.

10 published a study: Chaolin Huang, Yeming Wang, Xingwang Li, Lili Ren, Jianping Zhao, Yi Hu et al., "Clinical features of patients infected with 2019 novel coronavirus in Wuhan, China", *The Lancet*, 24 January 2020.

15 "any requirement": Section 477, *Biosecurity Act 2015*. See also Paul Karp, "Coronavirus: What power does the government have over you in a crisis?" *Guardian Australia*, 3 March 2020.

16 Imperial College London: Imperial College COVID-19 response team, *Report Nine: Impact of non-pharmaceutical interventions to reduce COVID-19 mortality and healthcare demand*, 16 March 2020.

16 Paul Kelly, suggested: Deputy Chief Medical Officer Paul Kelly, press conference, 16 March 2020.

16 Doherty Institute modelling: Brett Worthington, "Scott Morrison warns Australians to stay home for Easter or risk coronavirus horror scenarios", *ABC News* (online), 7 April 2020.

17 "Pandemic planning": Raina MacIntyre, Evidence before the Senate inquiry into the government's management of COVID-19, *Hansard*, 25 June 2020.

17 "I actually think": Peter Collignon, Evidence before the Senate inquiry into the government's management of COVID-19, *Hansard*, 25 June 2020.

30 put a safety net: Evidence to the Senate select inquiry into COVID-19, 28 April 2020.

32 "orderly and calm": Scott Morrison, press conference, Parliament House, Canberra, 22 March 2020.

33 "things of that nature": Morrison, press conference, 22 March 2020.

36 0.1 per cent: International Monetary Fund, press release, "Remarks by IMF Managing Director Kristalina Georgieva to G20 on Economic Impact of COVID-19", 22 February 2020.

37 "large, short-run economic impact": Steven Kennedy, Jim Thomson and Petar Vujanovic, "A primer on the macro-economic effects of an influenza pandemic", Treasury Working Paper, 1 February 2006, https://treasury.gov.au/sites/default/files/2019-03/TWP_01_2006.pdf.

39 "a cash splash": "Cormann rules out Rudd-style cash splash to boost Australian economy as coronavirus bites", *Guardian Australia*, 6 March 2020.

40 counselled Morrison: Confirmed to the author during a background briefing by the government, March 2020.

55 helpful organising thoughts: "L.Arthur Sinodinos on Scott Morrison's discipline and the future of the Liberal party", *Australian Politics Live* podcast, *Guardian Australia*, 2 November 2019.

56 "Australians have their own tribes": "On their side", Scott Morrison's address to the Liberal Party of Australia federal council, 24 June 2017.

60 displayed only limited interest: Malcolm Turnbull, *A Bigger Picture*, Hardie Grant, Melbourne, 2020.

61 "but it was a core part": John Kunkel, "Reflections on the Howard Project." *IPA Review*, May 2008.

69–70 "They transformed": Scott Morrison, Maiden speech to parliament, *Hansard*, 14 February 2008, pp. 348–53.

72 "psyche-up sessions": Sarah Martin, "Scott Morrison: 'Master of the middle' may pull Coalition out of a muddle", *Guardian Australia*, 21 April 2019.

77 Lijian Jhao: Lijian Zhao, Twitter, 13 March 2020.

77 "a beggar nation": George Packer, "We are living in a failed state", *The Atlantic*, June 2020.

78 "Waning American leadership": Richard Haas, "The pandemic will accelerate history rather than reshape it", *Foreign Affairs*, 7 April 2020.

79 "exerted a religious pull": Trump quoted in Julian Borger, "Donald Trump denounces 'globalism' in nationalist address to the UN", *Guardian Australia*, 25 September 2019.

79 people under thirty: Michael Safi, "Have millennials given up on democracy?", *Guardian Australia*, 19 March 2016.

81 only a quarter: Daniel Hurst, "Only 23% of Australians trust China to act responsibly in the world, Lowy Institute poll finds", *Guardian Australia*, 24 June 2020.

82 "depends on our dedication": Scott Morrison, 2019 Lowy Lecture, 3 October 2019.

84 "leaving others": Payne quoted in Daniel Hurst, "Australia accuses China of spreading 'fear and division' as diplomatic tensions escalate", *Guardian Australia*, 16 June 2020.

84 "smaller, more agile countries": Michael Fullillove, "Coronavirus: Global giants stumble while agile nations inspire", Lowy Institute commentary, first published in *The Australian*, 6 April 2020.

85 Commonwealth Bank: "An early look at how Covid-19 is affecting household spending", Commonwealth Bank research note, 30 March 2020.

86 spiked 50 per cent: Australian Bureau of Statistics, Media release, "Retail sales data for March", ABS, Canberra, 22 April 2020.

86 "extinction event": Craig Silverman, "The coronavirus is a media extinction event", *BuzzFeed*, 23 March 2020.

88 spat at: "Racism on the rise as Asian Australians made scapegoats for Covid-19", *Ten Daily*, 23 April 2020.

88 cyber-stalked: Shalailah Medhora, "eSafety office records 340% spike in complaints as coronavirus impacts behaviour online", *Hack*, Triple J, ABC, 22 April 2020.

88 terrible spiral: John Siddle, "Coronavirus: Teen dies after suicide attempt during isolation", News.com.au, 26 March 2020.

88 neighbourhood oval: Dan Jervis-Bardy, "Coronavirus ED to be built on Garran oval", *The Canberra Times*, 9 April 2020.

89 Guardian Essential polls: "Guardian Essential poll: One-third say there has been an over-reaction to the coronavirus", *Guardian Australia*. 24 March 2020; "Australians becoming more anxious about coronavirus threat, Essential poll finds", *Guardian Australia*, 31 March 2020; "Australians' trust in government and media soars as coronavirus crisis escalates", *Guardian Australia*, 7 April 2020.

89 "it deteriorated": Peter Lewis, "Trust in the government is rising but will Australians accept the coronavirus app?", *Guardian Australia*, 21 April 2020.

89 "up 11 per cent": "Half of Australian voters think it's too soon to consider easing lockdown, Essential poll finds", *Guardian Australia*, 21 April 2020.

91 "pandemics and plagues": Wade Davis, "The unravelling of America", *Rolling Stone*, 6 August 2020.

THE COAL CURSE

Correspondence

Zoe Whitton

Judith Brett's *The Coal Curse* is an insightful overview of Australia's struggle to develop industries beyond commodity exports, and the effect this concentration has on our national discourse and policy-making. It is a rare treat to read a deep case study of the resource curse in action, even if it is a little depressing to be reading it about one's own country.

Two features of our predicament, as outlined by Brett, stand out for me. First, the idea that our lopsided success might be challenging our ability to develop new strengths and growth opportunities. Brett doesn't suggest there is a causal link between our strength in extracting and exporting resources and our weakness in other industrial sectors, but she does note a number of ways they interrelate. One of these is that the resources industry breathes in people and capital as commodity prices rise and exhales them as they fall, challenging the growth of other sectors. The effect of our resource exports on other exporters via exchange rates is another.

This dynamic is reminiscent of the failure to innovate often observed in incumbent corporations. Why, so often, do strong organisations, dominant in their industry and aware of oncoming disruption, fail to respond and therefore get damaged or swept aside? Such companies tend to have high-powered and experienced boards, well-resourced strategy departments, and established customer relationships and infrastructure. They should be best positioned to seize new opportunities and see off attackers. Nonetheless, over and over again we observe such companies being overwhelmed and diminished by change. Why?

One proffered reason is the power of the existing successful business units within the organisation. Often an incumbent business unit negotiates so hard on all fronts that up-and-coming units don't get a look in. Once leadership is established around a dominant activity, it becomes difficult to allocate resources and time to anything else. This dominance can play out in myriad tiny decisions.

Should we spend our time and attention developing a new initiative which might fail, or should we double down on our most profitable activities? Should we change our governance slightly so that our new business unit can grow, or should we keep the existing structure which favours the dominant unit? Should we allocate growth capital to our new products, or to the products which presently make up the majority of our revenues? Each choice to back the status quo often makes sense in the short- or mid-term, and is hard to press back against. But over time they lead cumulatively to an inability to do much that is new.

How this translates is clear. Australia is extremely good at certain activities. We derive a significant portion of our income from those activities. We have experienced and capable leadership, resources to spare, and a reputation for delivery. But we have struggled to figure out how to become good at anything other than varieties of what we are presently good at (except in a few cases).

Where a company often struggles to spend the surplus from a dominant business on an upstart, Australia has struggled to tax established sectors to support the development of others. Where a company struggles to change incentives to favour a new unit, so we struggle to modify our national policy and norms to make space for the future. Our dominant industries often argue that they shouldn't be taxed as heavily or should be supported because they contribute so much to the national economy. (Brett outlines how the narrative efforts of our dominant industries have been hugely successful in this respect.) This conversation is almost a direct mirror of that sometimes seen between business units.

I should note that not all companies have this problem. Cases in which an organisation completely fails (usually by being consumed by others) are actually fairly rare. Many companies manage to survive their incumbency. Nonetheless, each decade provides a steady flow of new examples. Furthermore, incumbents often survive by buying upstarts – a common practice for companies, but more controversial when attempted by countries.

The second notable feature of our predicament is the difficulty we experience regarding climate change and the industrial transition it entails. As Brett notes, our national debate on the topic has become deeply polarised, often seeming to pertain mainly to our national identity and relevance rather than really discussing the challenge. To many people, our national conversation on climate change appears to have become somewhat deranged – full of sound and fury, and largely unrelated to the issues at hand. This is likely due in part to the challenges faced in all modern political conversations: the extent to which our media now operate by soundbite and clickbait; the increasing polarisation of our news infrastructure; inequality and its many ills. However, when it comes to climate change, there is probably something else afoot.

When viewed up close, the deterioration of our debate seems like a specific failure. It appears that a number of determined individuals in a specific set of industries may have bumped us off an otherwise constructive path, setting us into the melee which we now experience. However, seen from a distance, our trajectory looks more predictable and less personal. Some have long expected that Australia will necessarily fail to navigate a transition because even *thinking* about it will prove too difficult for us.

Why would this be so? Following Hurricane Sandy, British environmental campaigner George Marshall undertook a series of interviews with residents of the New Jersey seashore. He noted that those who lived through the unusually severe, life-threatening storm were less likely to believe in climate change than before. Why? Marshall gathered evidence about the issue for his 2014 book *Don't Even Think About It: Why Our Brains Are Wired to Ignore Climate Change*. His findings suggest that the desire to return to something like normal, to rebuild anew, and to express solidarity and perseverance prompted people to resist the prospect that the same disaster could happen again. The fact that climate change might be extremely threatening (it could destroy your house or kill you) makes conceiving of it even more difficult. More evidence of how threatening climate change might actually make it even harder to come to terms with.

Some commentators expect the same from us as a nation. At a conference in 2019, energy finance analyst Kingsmill Bond presented an analysis of which countries might move more quickly through a climate transition, and which might instead be overcome by it. The audience was a global group, interested primarily in the fortunes of Europe, the United States and eastern Asia, where they were based. Bond noted almost as an aside that a few (energy-exporting) nations would of course find it almost impossible to undertake a transition. He noted that the political and economic negotiations needed to undertake decarbonisation would likely prove too challenging for these states to navigate successfully, given their interests. However, he argued that the trajectories of these countries were irrelevant. There were only a few of them, and their populations were small. The rest of the world's population (largely living in countries which are net energy importers) would stand to benefit, and that was where the action would be in any case. The discussion moved on. I don't need to tell you which group Australia was in.

The discussion reminded me of a similar one we regularly have in the investment community. We often find ourselves pondering why some companies find it such a struggle to develop a climate change strategy, or even to discuss the topic. Why are they defensive, even when many proactive options are available to them? A common answer is that acknowledging a threat sometimes requires choosing between options that all seem less appealing than the status quo. Even when the status quo is not sustainable beyond the short term, the alternatives can seem so unappealing that we choose not to consider them. In these cases, it often feels preferable to kick the can down the road. Many companies have reason to feel threatened by climate change, but some companies may feel that none of the options available to address the threat are in any way desirable. In these cases, avoiding the discussion (or even pretending the threat doesn't exist) might feel more viable than looking at the danger straight-on.

Of course, we know that such companies, the reluctant nations Bond referred to and Marshall's post-disaster communities are far from alone in struggling to come to terms with the fear of far-reaching and threatening change. Furthermore, one can imagine that for individuals, companies and countries, a larger and more existential threat might generate even greater reluctance.

Our commodity-exporting industries certainly have the emotional resonance needed to generate this type of attachment. Growing up in a Queensland mining family (a splinter group of an agricultural family at that), I know what it is to feel the ebb and flow of commodities industries almost viscerally. As the mining industry grew throughout my childhood, it felt as though Queensland did too – our wealth, our perception of ourselves in the world, and our confidence. I remember the luxury stores that opened their doors on Queen Street as the mining boom took flight. Alongside the growing number of stately modern headquarters dotted around town, these felt like glittering markers of our new place in the world. This was a temporary feeling – a giant breathing in, if you will. The same stores have now been aged by time as much as by finding themselves in a different economic context. But as a teenager, it felt as if our world and our esteem was expanding with the industry.

Perhaps, coming from that place and time, I am more inclined to read into this emotional resonance. But in the mining community in Queensland during the boom, the industry and the future and Us felt tightly wound – one and the same. What threatened one, threatened all. Feeling attached like this makes it difficult to think with any objectivity about things which threaten the industry. And when it comes to an energy transition, this emotional resonance might be enough to make one's stance on transition a foregone conclusion.

Maybe as a consequence of these challenges, the Australian debate on transition has one more striking quirk, which is that we tend to speak about global change as if it's something we control. Specifically, we speak about the industrial transition of others as if our choices will change theirs. As if our policy decisions will change what Asia, Europe or the United States does. This is risky for two reasons. First, we don't get to choose whether climate change happens or not – or what the impacts are. Second, we don't get to choose whether others respond to climate change or not, nor how they do so. What we decide to do on climate change matters, but possibly not for the reasons we think. We discuss climate change and international agreements as if pulling out of them will change something, or (even more hopefully) break a spell and convince the world that it was all a fantasy. This is magical thinking at its most fantastic and dangerous. Instead, what we do matters because it will determine how fast and successfully we respond to the challenge, and how the rest of the world treats us as it moves forward.

On the first point (speed and success), there is an industrial revolution presently afoot, and we have the natural and intellectual resources needed to succeed. However, we will not win this game if we refuse to get on the field. On the second point, if our choices take us in a different direction to others, then they are very likely to impose a variety of costs on us to ensure they don't end up bearing our costs. Border-adjusted carbon prices are a good example of this – a policy mechanism under which a region can levy tariffs on imports which originate in jurisdictions without sufficient carbon constraints. These types of mechanisms allow regions to protect themselves and their industries – to transition without exposing their own economies to uneven competition. They might in some scenarios be used to protect these regions from us – from our high-carbon economy.

If we make certain choices, we may find ourselves playing a different game to large parts of the global economy, and paying for it on a number of fronts (including missed opportunities). We will miss the opportunity to win the game they are presently playing – one we are well set up to win. This is why it matters what we do – because it determines whether we're on the field, or not. To miss the commercial layer of this conversation is at best to be incumbent, complacent and a bit distracted. At worst, it is to be unbelievably naive in the service of our own hope and nostalgia.

Given this, why is there reason for hope? First, although there are many famous examples of entities which failed to navigate their own incumbency, there are also many which succeeded. Companies that, understanding their own mental blocks, targeted the futures they wanted. In order for these futures to be in play for us, we will have to do as these successful incumbents did – explicitly work our way through our challenges, knowing that our mental gravity will pull us back. Tie ourselves to the mast, if you will.

There are signs of hope in a number of recent policy projects. Though it has not been much discussed, the first half of the COVID-19 Commission's draft recommendations focuses very usefully on which advanced manufacturing activities might be built out in Australia. The Technology Investment Roadmap focuses on innovating through the problem and building new strengths and industries. CSIRO's new national missions aim to focus and protect innovation for specific outcomes. Beyond these policy efforts, we have the resources and expertise to solve the problem. As with incumbents, there is no reason it shouldn't be us that disrupts us – we merely (!) have to set ourselves on the path, find some rope, and perhaps use a little figurative wax to drown out the complaints of our established sectors.

A second cause for hope comes from outside Canberra, from the rest of Australia. I have framed the above discussion as if "we" are one entity. One community struggling to perceive the challenge, one group grappling with a single set of hopes and desires. This is, of course, not the case. Indeed, much of the furore I have described above is happening not in all of Australia, but in a much smaller, tighter arena, comprising Canberra and a collection of commentators. This arena is certainly extremely powerful. However, it is also a small and shrinking part of the national discussion on transition, likely because it has been so unwilling to engage on the topic to date and so has been effectively sidelined. Outside this arena, a growing majority of decision-makers are already putting in the work to navigate a transition.

When discussing the transition, many commentators elevate the importance of this small arena, equating a failure of federal transition policy with the failure of the nation as a whole. In some respects, this is true – overarching federal policy would speed up our response to the challenge and reduce the extent to which we make problems for ourselves in the future. It would boost our ability to compete in the game of our lives, ensuring that our footing is strong and that all our limbs are running together and in the right direction. It would make investment and action easier, faster, more competitive and more coordinated.

However, if Canberra fails on this issue – if our national leadership fails to ward off its own sirens – we still have many avenues for action. As Brett notes, every state or territory in Australia is presently committed to align with Paris. Many of our largest companies are decarbonising at a rate of knots (including some of our resource majors). Citizens, investors, regulators and companies alike are grappling with a transition – negotiating ways to hold one another to account, to invest despite uncertainty, and to innovate in the right direction with little assistance.

These decision-makers are pushing together towards the growth that we need to take the game (although, I will grant you, they argue every step of the way). When viewed as a whole, Australia looks very different to when viewed as Canberra. Recent history would suggest that our challenge will actually be addressed beyond Canberra and by other actors. Much of the action in Australia is now moving steadily in the right direction, despite the noise. As a major commodity exporting nation – and a major energy exporter – Australia faces a transition path which will be unlike those of many other developed economies. Nonetheless, it's possible for our path to be one of growth. To achieve this pathway, we must remember that we're more than just the apparently intractable fights which presently dominate our political conversations, and that we're capable of functioning despite being threatened by change. Like a family living in a cyclone-hit delta, we cannot just rebuild the same house our grandparents lived in. Nor the one our parents lived in. To thrive in our distinct part of the world with our distinct history, we will have to innovate, tie ourselves to the proverbial mast, and build something that is designed for our future rather than only our past. Many of us are already building it.

Zoe Whitton

THE COAL CURSE

Correspondence

Andy Lloyd

Professor Brett's dismay at the recent bushfires and lack of action on climate change is well founded. As a firefighter, I share her concerns. But Brett has been very selective in citing the activities of a few individuals in the mining industry on native title and climate policy, and accordingly she provides a very narrow view.

I am reluctant to defend the coalmining industry, because it should have done more itself to address its poor reputation. However, having worked in the industry for several decades and represented Rio Tinto in numerous industry associations in Australia and internationally, I wish to offer a very different perspective.

Professor Brett describes the negative response of much of the mining industry to the *Native Title Act 1993*, which at the time was highly contentious. In 1995, Leon Davis, the managing director of CRA, the Australian arm of Rio Tinto, made a landmark speech supporting native title and recognising the advantages of working in partnership with Aboriginal people. For mining companies, this would result in improved access to Aboriginal land, increased local employment options and greater security of tenure for mining projects, in addition to the obvious benefits for Aboriginal people. Professor Brett says the companies "could afford to be generous once they had won," but the reality is they were driven by the social and commercial imperative to do business in a manner that delivered effective outcomes for themselves and affected Aboriginal groups alike. The outcomes for Aboriginal people since then have been positive where agreements negotiated for development on Aboriginal land have aligned the interests of Aboriginal communities and mining companies by sharing the proceeds of development through royalties, employment, business development and other benefits, while protecting Aboriginal rights and interests in land, environment and cultural heritage.

Mining companies recognised emerging climate concerns by the late 1990s, and since then have sought to reduce greenhouse gas emissions despite the lack of clear government policy. While there has been vigorous debate and disagreement on exactly what to do, mining companies have responded to the emerging imperatives of climate change. On no occasion within the Australian coal industry can I recall climate science, as distinct from policy, being seriously debated, let alone dismissed. Rather, the starting point for these discussions was always that climate change was a significant problem that needed to be addressed. One that posed a challenge not just for the mining industry, but for every industry with high-energy inputs.

The idea of an all-powerful fossil-fuel lobby stalking the corridors of power, casting doubt on climate science and sabotaging national efforts to reduce emissions, is hilarious to most people inside these companies. It would also be news to politicians who have been directly involved in climate policy over this period and who have allegedly been "captured" by this lobby. Rather, Australian domestic climate policy over the past two decades can be explained almost entirely by a single question: what impact will this policy measure have on the cost and reliability of energy for domestic and business consumers? A closely linked question is: what impact will it have on Australian competitiveness?

Professor Brett uses the term "fossil-fuel lobby" in a way that implies everyone involved in the production of fossil fuels (the coal, gas and oil industries) rejects climate science and has worked to undermine emissions policy. This is patently false. All of the major public companies in these sectors long ago acknowledged the problem and have in place programs to reduce their own emissions. Many, including coal producers, have been working for decades on strategies to reduce emissions from the use of their products. For example, the black coal industry contributed over 20 per cent of the abatement achieved under the voluntary Greenhouse Challenge Program initiated in 1995 by the Keating government.

If there is an anti–climate science, pro–fossil-fuel lobby in Australia, it comprises a small number of politicians and commentators, not companies actually involved in the fossil-fuel industry. If these politicians have been "captured" by so-called fossil-fuel interests, then those interests do not include major producers.

If indeed there has been a sinister lobby working behind the scenes, sowing the seeds of climate denial and sabotaging emission reduction efforts in Australia, then it has been spectacularly unsuccessful. This is particularly true when it comes to coal. As Brett herself notes, ten coal plants have closed in Australia in the past ten years. No new ones have been commissioned for over a decade, and Australia is installing renewable energy (solar photovoltaics and wind) faster per capita than almost any other country. Our deployment rate is four to five times faster than in the European Union, United States, Japan and China.

The black coal industry recognised the challenges facing coal in the late 1990s, when it joined the Greenhouse Challenge Program and began to invest in abatement projects. By 2001, these challenges were made even clearer from its dialogue with the International Energy Agency. In 2006, the black coalmining industry in Australia agreed to create the COAL21 Fund to develop low-emission technologies, and all Australian black coal producers agreed to contribute to this fund. To date, the fund has invested nearly $400 million in emerging low-emission technologies. Numerous major technical research and demonstration projects have been undertaken, including oxy-firing of a conventional coal power station, pre- and post-combustion capture, in conjunction with work by the Cooperative Research Centre for Greenhouse Gas Technologies on carbon capture and storage (CCS).

The International Energy Agency itself has highlighted the importance of CCS in reducing emissions, and the Intergovernmental Panel on Climate Change, the organisation that reviews and distils the research of thousands of climate scientists, has consistently and repeatedly identified CCS as one of the critical technologies necessary to address climate change.

In about 2002, Rio Tinto joined with numerous other coal and oil and gas companies in the CO2CRC, which was established under the Australian government's Cooperative Research Centres (CRC) program. Its aim was to research and demonstrate CCS as a major industrial emissions-reduction technology. In 2012, Rio Tinto further expanded its contributions to the CO2CRC, providing $3 million over three years as part of the formation of the Peter Cook Centre for CCS Research. At the conclusion of CRC funding in 2014, CO2CRC Limited was established as a private, not-for-profit research organisation and to this day it owns and operates a major carbon storage research facility with more than $100 million invested in understanding how carbon dioxide behaves underground. In 2009, Prime Minister Rudd committed over $100 million to support the creation of the Global CCS Institute, which has carried forward this work internationally.

The efforts of the Australian coal industry to develop CCS are often incorrectly characterised as a failure. Further, many describe those efforts as a cynical external-relations tactic to cultivate the promise of future low-emission coal use while allowing business as usual for as long as possible. Any informed analysis exposes both notions as erroneous.

The knowledge developed by those early projects has supported the development of this technology elsewhere by nations and companies with budgets far larger than Australia's. In reality, the ambition of the Australian coal industry was a decade too early. The cost of capturing carbon dioxide from coal-fired power stations has halved since the COAL21 fund was launched in 2006. Two coal plants with CCS are operating (since 2014 and 2017) and in the past few months six more have commenced feasibility or FEED studies in the United States. These are not academic exercises. These are real projects with the intent of putting steel in the ground. If the coal industry was truly just conducting an external-relations exercise, or just continuing business as usual, it would not have spent hundreds of millions of dollars through the COAL21 Fund trying to support the development of a technology well beyond its core competencies. Nor would individual coal companies have spent tens of millions of additional dollars on their own CCS programs. Rather, the coal industry would have saved its money and instead focused its messaging on local efforts to reduce its own emissions and on its contribution to the community and economy, safe in the knowledge that the export coal market will be robust for decades.

The industry's actions were and are motivated by a desire to make a material contribution towards defeating climate change, while recognising the realities of the ongoing demand for coal, especially in rapidly growing Asia. Without CCS, it is, at best, twice as expensive to meet climate targets, and at that cost it is practically impossible. The actions of the industry are well removed from the climate denialism depicted by Professor Brett.

Around half of Australia's coal exports is metallurgical coal used for steelmaking. The other half is thermal coal used in power plants, with a small portion used to make cement, alumina, synthetic rutile and manganese. If it is true (and it is) that countries that import our thermal coal could readily source the same quantity elsewhere, why do they prefer the Australian product? The answer is that it generally has a higher energy content and a lower ash content, meaning it is more efficient and also lower in other important pollutants, such as sulphur and mercury. For India and China, which are determined to electrify their economies by whatever means available, and which already have an air pollution problem, this is an important consideration. Using Australian coal results in lower carbon emissions per unit of energy and fewer pollutants of other kinds. This does not make Australian coal "clean," just cleaner.

While the idea that support for Australian coal exports can only be logically explained by politicians being somehow "captured" by climate-denying fossil-fuel interests might make for a ripping yarn, the reality is far more prosaic. Most people understand the economic and environmental reasons why countries prefer to use Australian coal. And all understand the jobs, investment and national wealth to be foregone if Australia were simply to cede these markets to eager global competitors with no environmental benefit.

Apart from this, critics like Brett need to ask: if we want to be consistent and stop our emission-intensive exports, where do we draw the line? Cattle cause methane emissions, so Australia shouldn't export beef or dairy products? Aluminium production is responsible for emissions, so we shouldn't export bauxite? International tourism causes airline-related greenhouse gas emissions, so Australia should tell travellers to go elsewhere? The answer is to reduce greenhouse gas emissions across all sectors of the economy, including, of course, the more intensive emitters such as coal-fired power, both in Australia and internationally.

We need to demand that our politicians embrace the target of net zero emissions by 2050 and take effective action to meet that target. Certainly, we should be demanding greater efforts from the emission-intensive polluters, including the coalmining and coal-consuming industries, to invest in the development and deployment of low-emission technologies. We must demand action domestically, and we should also use our trading relationships to ensure that sales of Australian products come with commitments to invest similarly to reduce emissions.

New technology needs significantly more investment and Australia should play its part in an international effort. Developers of these technologies assume a significant financial risk, which is made more difficult in the absence of an economically efficient mechanism to reward cuts in emissions. The success of renewables is commendable, but we need as many emission-reduction options as possible, so that we can choose the most cost-effective options across all sectors of the economy.

As a firefighter, I share Professor Brett's dismay about climate change and the inadequate response to date. However, emergency management principles require that we remove emotion from our decision-making. If we believe in the climate crisis, it is hard-headed science and economics that we need to bring to bear. Even if we don't (yet) believe there is a climate crisis, we should act regardless, as the long life of polluting assets and the long lead times for new technologies mean that turning around our emissions will take decades. Demonising any one product or process distracts from this wider imperative.

Andy Lloyd

Correspondence

Peter Christoff

In *The Coal Curse*, Judith Brett eloquently describes how policy failures related to globalisation in the 1980s and 1990s enhanced our current dependence on fossil fuels. But she perhaps underestimates the role of the mining industry in hindering economic diversification and accentuating the dilemmas now faced by Australian governments grappling with climate change.

The mining industry learnt early on to promote and defend itself. In 1967, it formed the Australian Mining Industry Council (later the Minerals Council of Australia) to champion its interests. It resisted attempts under Whitlam to govern foreign investment through a Petroleum and Minerals Authority and, as Brett notes, undermined successive legislative iterations of land rights in the 1970s – and then again in the 1990s, following Mabo and Wik. It crushed Kevin Rudd's attempt to establish a resource super-profits tax in 2010.

The disciplinary effect of these successes cannot be overstated. But moments of direct challenge were relatively rare because there was a deep consonance of views, values and interests among politicians, bureaucrats and industry executives about the economic role of the mining sector. Brett, following Guy Pearse, notes how the Australian Industry Greenhouse Network – the self-named "greenhouse mafia," representing coal and aluminium interests – scripted climate and energy policy-making in the 1990s. But "state capture" as blatant as this was rare and perhaps an anomaly. Instead, corporate influence over mining policy was both subtler and more deep-seated. Influential elite networks helped align state and national policy and mining sector interests in ways favourable to the latter – especially in the major mining states of Queensland and Western Australia. Senior bureaucrats and politicians moved – and continue to move – from government to positions of influence in the mining sector, and vice versa. Mining professionals were appointed to bodies such as the Foreign Investment Review Board (Sir William Pettingell in the 1970s). Senior bureaucrats accepted positions of high influence in the minerals sector (Sir Donald James Hibberd). Politicians became industry lobbyists (former Minister for Resources and Energy Martin Ferguson, who advised the Australian Petroleum Production and Exploration Association after leaving federal parliament in 2013).

In Treasury, Foreign Affairs and Trade, and other departments with responsibility for minerals and energy, a common culture prevailed, greatly enhanced by the neoliberal turn under Hawke and Keating. It was allergic to economic nationalism, fixated on international competitiveness, and favoured minimal regulation. As a consequence, successive Australian governments failed to extract significant value from mineral resource exports through taxes or royalties. Substantial potential public revenue was lost, often repatriated to overseas shareholders. Meanwhile, governments provided considerable subsidies and assistance in the form of tax concessions and access to state-owned infrastructure. (In 1974, the Fitzgerald report suggested the latter contribution far outweighed the value of mining taxes.)

Australia's taxpayer-funded fossil-fuel subsidies currently total more than $12 billion each year despite G20 leaders (including Australia) committing, in 2009, to "phase out and rationalize, over the medium term, inefficient fossil-fuel subsidies." Australian governments also provide regulatory relief by fast-tracking approvals, minimising environmental regulatory constraints, sometimes constructing roads, rail and ports, and reducing royalty requirements, as is being considered for Adani's Carmichael coalmine.

The failure of resource governance in Australia has served us poorly. Consider the small country of Norway, which ensured its share of North Sea oil was fully state-owned and state-developed. To this day, Norway retains a majority interest in that resource, and its rigorous economic nationalism underpins a massive sovereign wealth fund, which now sustains and insulates its high standard of living and supports a significant foreign aid program as well.

By limiting our budgetary capacity to foster national economic diversity and resilience in a globalised world, the mining sector's rent-seeking has diminished Australian development perhaps as much as, or more than, the resource curse. And it now makes attempts to stop being a fossil-fuel republic that much more expensive.

As gamblers know, even a long streak of luck eventually gives out. Climate change will inexorably bring the recent boom in coal and gas exports to an end. The UNEP Production Gap Report 2019 highlighted the chasm between the current volume of fossil fuels produced and what is required to meet Paris Agreement climate targets. This gap is largest for coal, and growing. By 2030, countries plan to produce 150 per cent more coal than is consistent with a 2°C pathway, and 280 per cent more than is consistent with a 1.5°C pathway. The gap is also substantial for oil and gas. Countries are projected to produce 43 per cent more oil and 47 per cent more gas by 2040 than is consistent with a 2°C pathway.

At the Clean Energy Council's 2020 summit in July this year, Fatih Birol, executive director of the International Energy Agency, commented that: "if [existing coal plants] operate for their normal economic lifetime ... an average coal plant has a lifetime of forty years or so ... it is impossible to reach our climate targets, even the modest ones."

Almost total decarbonisation of the global power sector must occur in less than two decades if global average warming is to be held to below 2°C, and much faster for 1.5°C. When this occurs – and it is a "when" – the transition will necessarily be accompanied by closure of the "production gap" through a profound decline in demand for fossil fuels, and markets for Australian coal and gas. Long-term investments will become stranded assets at every point in the chain of production to consumption. The longer this transition is delayed, the greater the likelihood of collapse rather than orderly exit, and that governments will need to pay for structural adjustment. The bigger they are, the harder they fall. Australia's export energy sector is now a behemoth rushing towards the precipice.

Since the 1990s, Australia has adopted deeply contradictory policies on energy and climate change. Australia's domestic uptake of rooftop solar is among the highest in the world and construction of large-scale solar and wind plants has accelerated, despite a still turbulent investment environment. Australian power generation using black coal has fallen since 2015, as have emissions from the power sector – a trend that will only accelerate.

However, Australian fossil-fuel exports have – until very recently – been completely siloed from both domestic energy and climate policies. Their entirely contradictory trajectory has been granted immunity from questioning, their unbridled growth supported equally by both the Coalition and Labor. It is here that Brett perhaps understates the political tensions and challenges now facing Australian governments.

Conservatives have argued that, based on its domestic emissions, Australia is an insignificant contributor to the global emissions problem. While this line is wrong in its own right – Australia emits 1.2 per cent of total global emissions, is ranked fourteenth among 196 emitting nations, and is one of the world's highest per-capita emitters – this defence fails utterly when our total contribution to global warming is considered. Australia's total carbon footprint – domestic and exported emissions combined – is around 3.6 per cent of total global emissions. Australia is the world's sixth-largest producer of CO_2 emissions overall. Its embodied emissions, exported in coal and gas, are at least two and half times its domestic emissions. Moreover, projected growth in Australian gas and coal exports – if realised – will see Australia's total (extraction-based) emissions nearly double by 2030 compared to 2005. The current size and projected increase in Australia's exported emissions overwhelms the ecological benefit of domestic action. It is clearly of global importance.

So far, the responses from the Coalition and Labor have been rigidly defensive. Some deny that an "export problem" exists, pointing out that only domestic emissions count toward the UN Framework Convention on Climate Change's accounting requirements. Imported emissions are the responsibility of the importing country; it is not the supplier's duty to mitigate emissions. Others argue that banning sales of Australian coal and gas will merely lead to supply substitution from elsewhere. Or that there is an ecological benefit: Australian coal is "cleaner" than that from other sources. Or that it is morally wrong to deprive developing countries of this vital energy resource. Or that governments shouldn't intervene, as markets will resolve the issue.

There are strong counterarguments to each claim. For instance, it is arguable that in fostering fossil-fuel exports Australia is in breach of the UNFCCC, which outlines clear responsibilities for parties to "anticipate, prevent and minimise the causes of climate change," and declares states have a responsibility to "ensure activities within their jurisdiction or control do not cause damage to the environment of other States or areas beyond the limits of national jurisdiction."

The cynicism of arguments that "if we won't sell it, others will" and "it's all the buyer's responsibility" is clear. Australians and shareholders benefit materially from export of a recognised harmful substance, and therefore are linked to the destruction these commodities cause (think of alternative, morally repugnant examples: asbestos, or toxic waste). But such political responses belie the depth of paralysis on this issue within the Coalition and Labor.

The Coalition is still riven by the battle between climate believers and denialists. By contrast, Labor is caught between its need to appease urban and regional electorates with apparently divergent interests; to deal with internal tensions generated by the CFMEU, the mega-industrial union that covers mining; to manage its neoliberal inheritance; and to reply to the challenge from the Greens. Brett rightly highlights how Bill Shorten's equivocation over the Adani mine was read by voters in the Galilee Basin as a sign of duplicity. Labor believes the 2019 election was lost in Queensland and New South Wales on the issue of coal and climate. Yet Anthony Albanese has continued this pattern of fence-sitting.

Adani remains a dilemma and the current crisis for the ALP is reminiscent of the uranium mining debate that contributed to the formation of the Greens. The fossil-fuel export problem is as urgent, and its deadly outcomes more certain.

An integrated view of Australia's climate responsibilities demands coherence between its domestic and export-oriented energy policies and practices. The climate crisis leaves no place for new coalmines or gas fields, or for maintaining the existing ones. It urgently requires a clearly articulated industry adjustment plan for winding down fossil-fuel exports. We have very limited time for implementation, even if we begin now. The political and economic impediments to doing so remain considerable and we face the danger that an informal conspiracy of silence will continue to blanket this larger concern. But the longer-term burdens of inaction – political, social, economic and ecological – will far outweigh the costs of breaching that silence.

Peter Christoff

Correspondence

Anna Rose

Judith Brett has offered Australians a great gift: a detailed understanding of how our country got so stuck in our response to climate change, and who we can hold responsible. Describing how coal and gas companies converted their financial power into political influence over the federal Coalition, Brett makes the invisible blatantly visible. The mess Australia is in today did not just *happen*. It was never *inevitable*. It came about through particular people's choices and actions, and through other people choosing to look the other way.

As a climate campaigner over the past twenty-three years, I've seen hordes of coal and gas lobbyists at Parliament House and at party conferences; the handshakes and backslaps and laughs. Like Brett, I've despaired at the revolving door between politics, the senior public service and fossil-fuel companies. But it's not too late to turn things around.

The final chapter of Brett's saga is still being written, by the actions that we take today. In the decade or so the world's leading scientists say we have left to limit irreversible climate change, I see two viable pathways to get Australia unstuck on climate: first, shifting the Coalition, and second, shifting money away from coal and gas.

As Brett outlines, the fossil-fuel lobby has been incredibly successful at "capturing" the Coalition and using it to protect its financial interests. But for how long can this success continue? More fires will burn in places previously thought safe. Seas will continue to rise. More houses will fall into the ocean. More desperate people will be driven to our shores seeking safety from conflicts driven by food and water shortages. Many in the Coalition know it's only a matter of time before their position must change. The rise of groups like Coalition for Conservation and Parliamentary Friends of Climate Action, which has six federal Liberal Party members, shows that internal climate champions do exist.

For the past two decades, trying to support internal change in the Coalition has not been a priority for climate NGOs. Until the 2019 election, the better strategy seemed to be to pressure the ALP to improve its climate policy and hope for its election. But that strategy debate is now moot: we have already entered the critical decade for action, and the Coalition is in power federally and in three states. The latest Newspoll shows Scott Morrison's approval rating at 68 per cent, and he is preferred prime minister at 58 per cent (over Labor leader Anthony Albanese at 26 per cent). It is probable we will be dealing with Coalition governments until at least 2025. We simply do not have time to find a path to change that does not include the Coalition.

Just like John Howard's gun reforms, climate policies are much more likely to stick if introduced from the right of politics than the left. If it can muster the courage to reduce political support or financial subsidies for coal and gas, the Coalition is far better placed than Labor to withstand the inevitable attacks from the fossil-fuel lobby and its allies in the Murdoch media. This has been demonstrated in the United Kingdom, where the Murdoch newspapers have largely supported the significant climate leadership shown by the Conservative Party.

There are signs of progress in the three Coalition-held states. NSW environment minister Matt Kean stood up at the Smart Energy Council's annual conference in December 2019 and linked bushfires to climate change, making the case for stronger support for renewable energy. He couldn't have picked a more appropriate moment: the room, in Sydney's Hilton Hotel, was literally filling with bushfire smoke. Now Kean is forging ahead with two huge renewable energy zones for regional New South Wales, and Tasmania and South Australia have made rapid progress on renewables under their moderate Liberal premiers. Tasmania has a set a world-leading target of 200 per cent renewables, and South Australia is aiming for 100 per cent renewables before 2030. Every state and territory now has a target of net zero emissions by 2050. Should they choose to do so, the state premiers could work together, bypassing the federal government, to accelerate the transition to clean energy.

But what about Coalition politicians from the centre-right (Scott Morrison's faction) or the far right? In 2011, I spent four weeks filming an ABC documentary with former Liberal finance minister Nick Minchin. After over a hundred hours in conversation with Nick, I understood why he and others in the far-right faction were so opposed to accepting climate science. The science itself wasn't the problem – rather, it was its implications for policy. This is what Professor Naomi Oreskes calls "implicatory denial": accepting climate change means accepting that the neoliberal project of free markets and small governments produced a seriously large externality (a cost not reflected in the market price of fossil fuels, paid by the community in the form of climate change). In the words of Sir Nicholas Stern, climate change is the "greatest market failure ever seen," and governments must step in to fix it. This calls into question the ideology that Nick Minchin and others like him have devoted their whole lives to advancing.

The political reality is that change inside the Coalition cannot happen until enough of these "climate blocker" politicians leave federal parliament to allow the rest to move forward, or unless the moderates increase their powerbase to render the blockers' opposition irrelevant. Ultimately, it seems unlikely that the Coalition will feel the urgency to act that the science demands unless the federal Liberal Party is at serious risk of losing seats over climate change. Independent Zali Steggall's successful campaign for the seat of Warringah was a turning point. It has inspired long-time conservative voters in other seats to take matters into their own hands and find and back pro-climate independents. Ironically, those whose heads are next on the chopping block are Liberal moderates in inner-city seats who do accept the science. These Liberal MPs – people such as Trent Zimmerman, Tim Wilson, Katie Allen and Jason Falinski – may argue that their presence in parliament is critical to transforming the Coalition's climate policy. But these moderates have been so unwilling to risk any political capital over climate policy to date that voters in their electorates may decide instead that electing pro-climate independents and hoping they gain the balance of power is a more viable pathway to change. Perhaps the threat to the moderate Liberal voter base will prompt them to become more effective internal champions for climate action.

Ultimately, this is why the Coalition shifted on marriage equality. The few genuine champions inside the Liberal Party worked in partnership with Coalition MPs who weren't personally passionate but who felt enough heat from their electorates that they understood they risked losing a generation of young voters. Climate campaigners have learnt from the marriage equality movement and are getting better at making climate change relatable through personal stories and more targeted work with conservative-leaning voters and constituency groups. There are now organisations focused on working with farmers, veterinarians and vet nurses, emergency leaders, bushfire survivors, parents, doctors, other health professionals, elite athletes, psychologists, engineers, lawyers, Aboriginal and Torres Strait Islander people, the Jewish community, various Christian denominations, ethnic communities in south and south-west Sydney, and retirees – to name just some. These groups understand that a "one size fits all" climate message hasn't worked. To be effective, messages need to be delivered by people trusted within these communities, using stories and data that resonate and inspire action. Targeted campaigns can also influence stakeholder groups that are traditionally aligned with, and trusted by, the Coalition. Journalists often point to the National Farmers' Federation's shift to supporting action on climate change as an example of how out of touch the Nationals are with their traditional backers. But the influence of groups like Farmers for Climate Action in shifting the position of the Farmers' Federation is less well known.

These new groups – which I refer to as "Climate Movement 2.0" – can change the information environment not just for voters, but also for politicians, their advisers, friends and families, donors, and the think-tanks and lobby groups they listen to and accept advice from. And they, like all of us, can focus their efforts not just on the politics, but also on business.

With the second pathway to change – shifting money from coal and gas – the headwinds are blowing less strongly. Brett describes the "shareholder and customer campaigns to divest from fossil fuels." Many of Australia's most strategic climate campaigners are now focusing their advocacy on banks, insurers and asset managers, such as superannuation funds. This simple but powerful tactic was described by author and 350.org co-founder Bill McKibben in an influential *New Yorker* article last year: "the key to disrupting the flow of carbon into the atmosphere may lie in disrupting the flow of money to coal and oil and gas." New fossil-fuel projects are the main driver of climate change, yet very few, if any, fossil-fuel companies can self-finance and self-insure. If they can't get loans, investment or insurance for their coalmine expansions or fracking wells, these projects simply can't proceed. As Brett notes, BlackRock's decision to offload its thermal coal shares and "put climate change at the centre of its investment strategy" was a key moment. Blackrock's CEO Larry Fink did not just wake up one day and have a moral epiphany: the company was the target of a concerted campaign by the Sunrise Project and other groups.

Banking, asset management (superannuation and other companies that aggregate and invest money) and insurance companies are in a powerful position in Australia, too. If the fossil-fuel industry's plans to extract more gas and coal from New South Wales, Queensland, Western Australia and the Northern Territory can't get insurance, finance or investment, they won't proceed.

Businesses in other sectors of the economy can also play a role, by leveraging their historical and ongoing relationships with the Coalition. It is much more acceptable within the Coalition to be influenced by, and seen to be influenced by, business than it is to be seen to be influenced by environmental groups. This means any business (particularly ASX200 companies, which have more economic and therefore political clout) has a platform and power that it can use to champion climate action. Or, if it doesn't voluntarily choose to do so, it can be encouraged to find its voice by the same customer, shareholder or employee activism that has been so influential with the banks, investors and insurers to date. All of us can play a role in this, through organisations that run effective corporate campaigns, such as Market Forces and the Australasian Centre for Corporate Responsibility. The ACCR, for example, aggregates 100 shareholders, including large institutional investors, every time it puts forward a shareholder resolution at a company AGM. These shareholder resolutions are the thorn in the side of companies such as BHP, Woodside and AGL. The ACCR played a key role in getting the Minerals Council to the point where it now has a climate policy – ACCR was demanding that BHP cease being a member.

As Brett writes, right now "Australia is at a crossroads," as the pandemic has paused so much of the world's economy. There is an opportunity in the National Cabinet, formed initially to respond to the pandemic, but now extended. Energy policy is on its list of issues to consider. With no Nationals in the National Cabinet, and all three Liberal premiers being moderates from states committed to net zero emissions by 2050, perhaps we will finally see the bipartisan progress on climate that most Australians crave.

Brett describes many points in Australia's economic and political history when things could have taken a different turn. A small group of determined people created the situation we are in today – to protect their profits and advance their ideology. There was no guarantee they'd win. The history of social movements across the world shows that groups of committed people, small and large, can overcome even the longest odds. Progress is happening on climate change within both the Coalition and corporate Australia. The key question for ordinary Australians is: how can we accelerate it in the time scientists tell us we have left?

As Martin Luther King Jr said: "Over the bleached bones and jumbled residues of numerous civilizations are written the pathetic words: 'Too Late'." And in the words of Antarctic explorer Robert Swan: "The greatest threat to our planet is the belief that someone else will save it."

Anna Rose

THE COAL CURSE

Correspondence

Tim Buckley

At the Institute for Energy Economics and Financial Analysis, we track patterns of investment in or divestment from fossil fuels. Despite, or maybe because of, the global pandemic, 2020 has seen significant momentum in the movement of global capital away from thermal coal and coal-fired power generation. This reflects the rapidly diminishing economic merits of coal, but also a growing understanding that a commitment to the Paris Agreement will render many coal projects stranded assets, unable to deliver sufficient return over their proposed life.

In April 2020, a record twelve global financial institutions upgraded their commitments to divest from coal. The geographic spread revealed the global nature of the shift: three were from Japan, three from Germany, two were Citi and Morgan Stanley of the United States – and this was rounded out by one each from South Africa, France, the UK and the Netherlands.

The two massive private Japanese banks, Mizuho Financial Group and SMBC, were significant, but the action of the public Japanese Bank for International Cooperation (JBIC) was really telling, given that it was the world's largest provider of government capital to coal-fired power plants outside of China in the previous five years. It reflected a fundamental shift in thinking at Japan's Ministry of Economy, Trade and Industry, which culminated in the announcement that Japan would close 100 of its oldest coal power units by 2030. This is a huge step: 22 to 24GW of end-of-life coal-plant closures, three times the last 6 to 9GW of proposed coal plants still under development in Japan. With this, Japan will move past peak coal capacity installed – a defining moment, and a critical milestone for Australian thermal coal exports as Japan is our largest coal export destination (45 per cent in total).

June and July 2020 have seen momentum continue to build. Fourteen globally significant financial institutions have introduced or tightened coal exclusion, divestment or restriction policies: Westpac, QBE Insurance, HESTA and First State Super (Australia); BNP Paribas, Societe Generale and Natixis (France); Toho Bank (Japan); CDC Group (UK); Intesa Sanpaolo (Italy); Norges Bank (Norway); Deutsche Bank (Germany); Credit Suisse (Switzerland) and MetLife (United States). May 2020 also saw BlackRock complete divestment from thermal coal-mines and put KEPCO (South Korea) on notice for continuing to invest in new coal power plants.

In total since 2015, we at the Institute have tracked 139 globally significant banks, insurers and asset managers or asset owners that have implemented substantial policies on coal. In 2020, there have so far been forty-eight new or updated policy statements.

There is growing recognition of the technology disruption of global energy markets, affecting oil and fossil gas demand as well as thermal coal for power generation. The seemingly unstoppable rise in the Tesla share price (up 400 per cent in the last five years) has made it the largest automotive company globally (by equity market capitalisation). This shows the energy disruption is increasingly affecting both the power and transportation sectors, as battery technology breakthroughs drive a sector convergence. And 2020 has seen a clear pivot in rhetoric from the European oil and gas majors. Leaders at Total, Shell, BP, Eni, Repsol and Equinor are now talking about the inevitable disruption, compelled by the need to align with the Paris Agreement. Rather than just words, we are seeing the start of a pivot, as these firms reduce capital investments in new fossil-fuel exploration and divert new investments into zero-emissions technologies. June 2020 saw Total agree to acquire a 51 per cent stake in the new business developing the £3 billion 1075 MW Seagreen offshore wind farm in Scotland. And July 2020 saw a new Shell/Eneco consortium win the 759 MW Hollandse Kust (Noord) offshore wind tender in the Netherlands. These are likely to be two of the largest renewable energy projects developed this year globally.

Judith Brett's *The Coal Curse* is spot-on: Australia is being held back by the enormous power and corrupting self-interest of the fossil-fuel-export industry, which has entirely captured our federal political process. There is a growing divide between the Australian states embracing technology-driven investment and employment opportunities with both hands, and the captured federal government, which is doing its utmost to lie, obfuscate and distract, trying in vain to hold back the tide. Technology will inevitably win this race, but Australia could be so much better prepared with real political leadership.

Tim Buckley

THE COAL CURSE

Correspondence

Stephen Bell

Judith Brett's fine essay highlights the tough going we are currently experiencing in trying to shift the structure of the economy away from heavy reliance on fossil fuels towards renewables and, perhaps, associated downstream industries. From the current travails, one would think Australians are no good at economic restructuring. In fact, we are: we've done it several times on a large scale, though it seems to take us a long time, mired, as always, in political contestation.

Our economy has been through at least two periods of major structural change. The Australian settlement at the turn of the twentieth century used tariff protection and a highly administered labour market to spur the growth of manufacturing so as to reduce reliance on the volatile global commodities markets and boost employment and population. It worked: by the 1960s, manufacturing accounted for almost a third of national employment and GDP. But the settlement came only after several decades of battles between free traders and protectionists and was eventually stitched together with the support of industrial capital and the labour movement.

The second major transformation came with the winding back of the manufacturing sector, which by the 1960s had become bloated and inefficient on the back of political largesse and world-beating levels of no-questions-asked protection. This battle started in the late 1960s, when the Tariff Board, headed by one of Australia's early neoliberals, Alf Rattigan, suddenly declared war on protectionism, using innovative economic analysis to show that the sector was inefficient, uncompetitive and costly.

We are now stuck in another battle over economic restructuring and it is useful to compare this one with the last. The battle against protected manufacturing was a titanic struggle. As noted, the sector was big, and it was defended vehemently by one of the most powerful politicians of the post-war era, John McEwen. McEwen was the deputy prime minister and leader of the Country Party, which had for decades crafted a vote-winning alliance between farmers and manufacturers on the basis of "protection all round," something that had become close to a national religion. Manufacturers and manufacturing unions would attempt to scare politicians with threats of disinvestment and job losses in a wide array of manufacturing electorates, across New South Wales, Victoria and South Australia in particular.

Yet the protectionist arguments put forward by the manufacturing sector were no match for the more sophisticated economic analysis coming from the Tariff Board and, later, the Industries Assistance Commission, as well as from a range of economists who started to quantify the high costs the sector was imposing on the economy. This cause was also supported by the media and by the broader shift towards neoliberal thinking that increasingly saw post-war protectionism as a failed experiment. Governments also supported change, with the Whitlam government's 25 per cent tariff cut in 1973, efforts by the Fraser government to pull down at least some tariffs, and then the main effort by the Hawke/Keating governments amid bipartisan political support to push ahead with fully reducing tariffs, even in the recession in the early 1990s. The sector was also hit by structural change in the world economy that saw northeast Asian manufacturing, in particular, become too competitive to withstand. These structural forces helped drive a prevailing sense of economic malaise by the 1980s – epitomised by the "banana republic" crisis – that galvanised the mood for change.

Yet our attempts at industry restructuring never "got manufacturing going again," as Treasurer Paul Keating had hoped. Instead, our efforts just about killed off the patient (manufacturing is now less than 6 per cent of GDP), leaving little in its place. The mining boom of the 1990s was fortuitous, but it provided a further hit to manufacturing through a higher commodities-powered dollar that once again engendered that "lucky country" feeling, lulling us into a false sense of security.

The current battle over restructuring and the confrontation with the "coal curse" is proving to be even tougher in some ways than the protection battle, mainly because this time the political resistance is stronger and more insidious. The coal and gas sector are far more politically mobilised and influential than the manufacturers probably ever were. This reflects the general ramping up of political activism by large corporates in Australia in recent decades. It saw the stunning victory of miners over the Rudd government's proposed mining tax. And, despite the relatively few workers employed in coal mining, it is reflected in the power of a number of coal electorates, especially in Queensland, supported by National Party politicians who have made a vocation out of climate denial and climbing into bed with the coal lobby, just as they have with large irrigators in the Murray–Darling Basin. Unfortunately, too, the climate wars and the battle over coal have become part of a wider political and ideological struggle between the hard right and progressives. This is even being fought out within the Liberal Party, with deposed prime minister Malcolm Turnbull likening his rightist enemies in the party to "climate terrorists." This "debilitating political polarisation," as Brett puts it, has killed bipartisanship and made change more difficult. The government has either actively supported or stood by while all this has been happening, while rightist think-tanks, radio shock jocks and the Murdoch press egg on climate denial and praise the wonders of coal. Brett calls this "state capture," but it's probably best seen as common cause between the key players involved, one that has uniquely, and on the international stage embarrassingly, skewed Australian politics.

Change is thus being stymied by a national lacuna around energy policy – other than the newfound fondness for gas – and by the lack of any restructuring or regional policies to support displaced workers and communities as part of a properly thought-out energy transition; the kind of policy framework that is also sadly lacking in the Murray–Darling Basin, where battles over water play out as the Basin dries out under climate change. Finally, unlike in the 1980s, there is less of a sense of national crisis spurring change. Moreover, from the 1990s, Australia seemed to learn that we could achieve strong macroeconomic performance and rising terms of trade without a strong manufacturing sector, riding a resource boom instead. In some ways, this was Australia's "prosperity curse": reassuring, but ultimately unreliable, masking underlying structural weaknesses that are now manifest.

Indeed, the trouble for this model is that just as Australia's manufacturing was hit by a structural crisis which ultimately forced change, so too now are dreams of Australia's future based on fossil fuels. The climate challenge is one such structural pressure, but another one, perhaps more important politically, is the falling cost of renewables, which Judith Brett documents. Ultimately, renewable energy technologies, market forces and investors will drive change. This will help loosen the "deadly grip," as Brett puts it, of climate deniers and fossil-fuel advocates and make the fossil-fuel sector increasingly redundant. This is happening faster than many could have imagined and will one day represent something of a reconciliation of the old binary of environment and economy.

We have lost more than a decade in the climate and coal battles thanks to misguided conservatives, the coal lobby and its supporters, and terrible national leadership from the Coalition. This has generated a fake climate policy, an energy policy that's a mess, and the Nationals screaming for a new coal-fired power station. Surprisingly, from this morass a bright future is still possible, but only if we reap the huge potential gains from Australia's comparative advantages in renewable energy, along the lines set out in Ross Garnaut's recent book, *Superpower*. If we can do this, the gains could be used to help the losers from the declining fossil-fuel sector, and, unlike our earlier attempts to restructure manufacturing, we might end up with a strong new sector based on abundant energy driving a range of new downstream industries, including a hydrogen economy. We might also be able to rescue our battered international climate reputation.

Stephen Bell

THE COAL CURSE

Correspondence

Russell Marks

History is not valued very highly in the disciplines of law I've practised in (criminal and mental health). What matters there is legislation, evidence (of individual culpability) and precedent, which is about as far as the discipline reaches into the past, though precedent is used less as "history" than as a kind of regulation or restraint on present thought. The historian in me is forever confounded by what I (and many others) see as criminal law's blinkered approach to offending behaviour –which, it insists, is best conceived of as individuals making bad choices in a sociocultural vacuum in which other disciplines of Western knowledge – sociology, psychology, economics or, indeed, history – have little of value to add. This blinkered worldview allows criminal law to function as a tool of real oppression in certain communities of socioeconomic disadvantage, and especially in Aboriginal communities, because criminal law studiously ignores what it doesn't want to see. This is a privilege common to many Western disciplines, though not, if they're done properly, to the arts (including history).

I've also learnt, through brief exposures to the federal and Victorian parliaments, that history is not valued much more highly in the practice of politics. What matters to politicians is power: how to win it, retain it, use it. This creates a tension for both reformers and defenders of the status quo, for whom power is a means to an end. If history has value in power politics, it's unsurprisingly an instrumental value, as evident in appeals to certain historicised narratives or claims to historically rooted identities or traditions. In *The Coal Curse*, Judith Brett shows us how successful such appeals have been when they've been made by those with an interest in mining Australia's coal and gas deposits.

For those of us who – unlike practically all Australia's most senior political leaders at Commonwealth, state and territory level – believe that Australia's future lies not in coal but beyond it, is history helpful? This is a political question – what is to be done, and how? – so the framing is already instrumental. Could a loose collective of "post-coal" activists make historically situated appeals to identity and values and culture and nation in a way that rivals and overcomes the mining lobby? Progressives in Australia have been notoriously bad at this kind of "cultural politics of nation" since they realised about fifty years ago that the "radical nationalist" politics they'd been prosecuting had relied on highly racialised (white), gendered (masculine) and settler-colonial assumptions about Australian identity, as expressed in what was known as the Australian Legend. Humphrey McQueen's *A New Britannia*, which did as much as anything to demythologise the Legend for the Left, turns fifty this year, but that politics hasn't gone away. As Brett herself once wrote, John Howard "raided the Australian Legend for the Liberal Party." Having long foregone this symbol of white Australia's past, progressives now tend to appeal to more cosmopolitan identities, or to reason. But the political culture of Canberra and the mainstream commercial media – that with power to make change, or not – isn't much taken with reason these days, as Brett demonstrates.

Perhaps history's value is in reminding us of the possibility that it could all disappear. For humans, the worst case for global warming involves the collapse of economic and social systems, or – worst of all – the environmental systems that support human life. Empires and civilisations have collapsed before. Climactic change is often implicated. What is impossible to know – what history doesn't tell us – is what individuals and communities were doing while structures were failing around them. I suspect much the same as we do in recessions: getting on with things until we can't. Although there is much that might be attempted now to find alternative ways of living that don't rely on feeding our economic system's insatiable demand for energy, most of us need to pay the bills. So we go on, getting and spending.

History reminds us that the coal lobby wasn't always in charge (which makes it possible to imagine a time when it won't be again), that earlier lobbies (pastoral, industrial) eventually collapsed, that temperatures have warmed in ways that were predicted, that the deposits being sold off to create billionaires are extracted from stolen land and exploited communities. This is the function of Brett's essay. But who reads this kind of history? Mostly, people who already agree that coal is causing environmental devastation and that the coal lobby is far too powerful. And almost certainly not those who have drunk the Coal-Aid, unless their aim is to lampoon it and its author, as the Murdoch stable is wont to do. This is the crisis of Australia's intellectual life: the apparent impossibility of generating a constructive, rational dialogue about anything in general, and about coal in particular. Some historians will remind me that this remark is hopelessly naive, that power politics are as old as humanity and that it was ever thus.

Perhaps constructive, rational dialogue has always been a democratic myth. Other schools of political thought, with instructors ranging from Machiavelli to Foucault, identify the key concept as power. The content of reasoned debate matters less than the power to frame what is reasonable. But the history of reform does allow a place for reason, as informed by ethics, imagination, intuition, memory and common sense. It could be said that reform depends on reason. Social reforms, such as the civil rights movements for women, people of colour and LGBTIQ+ people, have succeeded in part by explaining to heterosexual white men how their own axioms, such as that "everyone is equal," are meaningless unless universally applied. Environmental reform has built on scientific observation and logic. It is those with interests threatened by reform movements, such as the coal barons, who use well-worn tactics of obfuscation to muddy debate and sow doubt.

The coal lobby has been remarkably successful at convincing Australia's democratically elected political leaders that the relatively few jobs its industry creates are somehow more important than the many more jobs connected with other industries, like tourism, or with more life-sustaining occupations, like farming. As Brett shows, the lobby has also been remarkably successful at convincing Australia's political leaders that the costs of our present status as international pariah are less than those of divesting from coal. The path to reform isn't linear, or simple. Among those most afflicted by the curse of coal are now Aboriginal owners. Leading Indigenous academic Marcia Langton regularly points out that the mining industry, for all the harm it causes to environmental health and sacred sites, is now the leading supplier of jobs, training, compensation and economic development in many remote Aboriginal communities. The economy that would be lost from these communities if mining stopped is just one of many problems reformers must confront.

What can ordinary people do – how can we exercise our agency – to improve the chances that future historians write a story of civilisational reform and revitalisation rather than collapse and doom (indeed, that there are historians in our future)? One history that remains to be told is that of the divestment movement, which Brett mentions briefly at the end of *The Coal Curse*. Divesting from coal has made environmental sense for some time. There are now plenty of products available to financial consumers that keep our money out of coal. Some of them offer slightly higher fees or slightly lower returns than the coal-fired products. Each of us lucky enough to have assets is now being asked to forgo a small percentage of wealth in the interests of global health. Despite this, divestment has recently begun to make financial sense as well – for major investors, but also the rest of us who, through mortgages and superannuation, have a stake in stocks and bonds whether we want to or not. As the histories of most successful movements show, divestment has something of a self-fulfilling prophecy about it. The more divestment there is, the greater the risk that coalmines become stranded assets companies can't profit from and can't sell: a true curse. Even if ethics won't get those of us lucky enough to have substantial assets over the line, the ever-increasing risk profile of unethical investment in coalmining and exploration probably should.

Russell Marks

THE COAL CURSE

Response to Correspondence

Judith Brett

In late May, when my Quarterly Essay was at the printers, Rio Tinto blew up the Juukan Gorge in the Pilbara, destroying two sites sacred to the Indigenous owners and which held evidence of at least 46,000 years of human occupation. Outrage was immediate. Rio Tinto protested that it had received permission for the blast in 2013, under Western Australia's 1972 *Aboriginal Heritage Act*, and that it had consulted with the traditional owners, the Puutu Kunti Kurrama and Pinikura (PKKP) people. Just days before the explosives were detonated, lawyers for the traditional owners had contacted the federal minister for Indigenous affairs to ask the federal government to intervene. Rio Tinto immediately issued an apology, accompanied by a reminder of just how important it was to Australia's prosperity: "The mining industry supports all Australians by providing jobs, supporting small business, and paying taxes and royalties."

The exact course of events is currently being investigated by the Senate's Joint Standing Committee on Northern Australia, and Rio Tinto is suffering deserved reputational damage. Likely there will be changes to Western Australia's heritage legislation, and mining companies will be more careful in their consultations, but there will be no fundamental shift in the power imbalance between Indigenous owners and miners, nor between Indigenous understandings of the land as sentient and imbued with ancestral power and settler capitalism's view of it as a resource for economic exploitation.

The focus on the protection of heritage and sacred sites distracts from the fundamental incompatibility of these two understandings of the land. Speaking on behalf of another group of Pilbara traditional owners, the Wintawari Guruma Aboriginal Corporation, Dr Kathryn Przywolnik told the Senate inquiry, "Within two generations, Eastern Guruma people have seen their country change from a remote place teeming with wildlife, fresh water and unbroken sacred narratives that networked through the Pilbara, to a heavily industrialised mining hub, now dissected by railways, dry and devoid of animals." Ring-fencing sacred sites won't restore the Eastern Guruma people's country.

In his final report for the Aboriginal Land Rights Commission in April 1974, Mr Justice Woodward said: "I believe that to deny Aborigines the right to prevent mining on their land is to deny the reality of their land rights." Woodward's belief was captured in the Northern Territory land rights legislation, which gave Indigenous land-rights holders the right to free and informed consent to mining on their land, but, as I discussed in *The Coal Curse*, the mining lobby was successful in preventing requirement for such consent in other land rights legislation and in the 1993 *Native Title Act*.

The inquiry also heard from Dr Przywolnik that land marked for mining is dotted with rock shelters, camping sites, and painted and engraved rocks, as one would expect of an area occupied by humans for millennia. Many features have already been destroyed and many are in the path of planned expansions. With Australian export income more dependent than ever on iron ore, stronger ring-fencing is the best Indigenous owners can expect.

As mining positions itself as crucial to Australia's post-pandemic economic future, the pressure from the fossil-fuel lobby is unrelenting. Santos's Narrabri gas mine is on the cusp of being approved despite strong community opposition, and the taskforce on manufacturing set up by the federal government's hand-picked National COVID-19 Coordination Commission is urging the government to support a dramatic expansion of gas supply, with tax incentives and financial support for new projects. This is only necessary, remember, because so much of our domestically produced gas is needed to fill export contracts. This gas, the taskforce argues, will sustain and expand Australian manufacturing. The taskforce seems not to have considered the possibilities of rebuilding with renewable energy, despite the plans put forward by the Grattan Institute, the Greens, Beyond Zero Emissions and the Climate Council. The Australian Workers' Union is calling for the Queensland government to approve the expansion of the New Acland coalmine in the Darling Downs, as is the resources minister, Keith Pitt, and Labor's shadow resources minister, Joel Fitzgibbon. With the economy in freefall, the arguments are all about jobs, of course, and the need to reduce the green tape which, it is argued, hampers investment and development. The zero-sum game between the environment and the economy is still hardwired into the thinking of many Australians.

But, as Tim Buckley makes clear, there are strong counter-forces at work in the speed and scale of divestment from fossil fuels, partly driven by climate activists and partly by declining profitability as the price of renewable energy falls.

The share market's judgment on coal is grim, with the Dow Jones US coal index down 92 per cent from its peak in May 2018. Gas is holding up better, but still faces strong headwinds. Buckley's colleague at the Institute for Energy Economics and Financial Analysis Bruce Robertson reports that major gas companies are losing money. Of the COVID-19 Commission's enthusiasm for government support for gas, he says, "Governments are not meant to back winners, but they're certainly not meant to back losers."

Neoliberalism rejected the social democratic faith that governments should and could intervene in markets to produce desired social outcomes. When pressure from climate activists started, neoliberals believed that emissions reductions could only be achieved through top-down government intervention. Anna Rose writes that after spending time with Nick Minchin, who was instrumental in blowing up Malcolm Turnbull's leadership of the Opposition and its support for Kevin Rudd's emissions-trading scheme, she realised that his climate denialism was linked to his neoliberal belief in free markets and small government. Ironically, in Australia it is now the free market that is driving change, as householders install rooftop solar, businesses look to future risks and gifted entrepreneurs like Mike Cannon-Brookes and Sanjeev Gupta invest in ambitious renewable energy projects. Were we in an authoritarian state run by fossil-fuel tsars, this would not be happening.

Under Morrison, the Coalition government has been much less hostile to renewable energy than it was under Abbott. For example, it has just granted major project status to the Sun Cable project, which would export renewable energy to Singapore via undersea cable from a massive solar farm in the Northern Territory. This is the sort of project Ross Garnaut argued for in *Superpower*, in which the export of renewable energy replaces the export of fossil fuels.

Even so, the federal government still has no national energy policy, despite widespread stakeholder support for some form of emissions-trading scheme. And although quiet for now, the Coalition's climate deniers have not gone away. Rose's argument that climate activists need to target conservative groups and focus on shifting the Coalition is shrewd. The Coalition is in government, time is running out, and the policies it introduces are more likely to stick. As we have seen in the past wasted decade, the Coalition has deep reserves of self-righteous anger always to hand to attack Labor and the Greens, as well as the willingness to destroy good policy for purely political ends. A similar argument can be made about the government's massive spending to support people and businesses through the lockdowns. If Labor were in government, would the Coalition be supportive, or would it revert to its customary attack on Labor as the irresponsible party of tax and spend?

Zoe Whitton writes eloquently about the visceral emotional attachment of Queenslanders to mining, which makes it difficult for many to think rationally about the industry's threatened future. Like Buckley, she believes that an unstoppable technological revolution is underway and that the days of fossil-fuel extraction are limited, whatever our governments do. Although innovation in renewable energy began from the need to drive down emissions, it now has a financial momentum as it out-competes coal, and this is exposing structural weaknesses in Australia's poorly diversified economy. As Stephen Bell says, these were masked by the prosperity of the mining boom.

Most days I scan the business pages of the major dailies for stories about coal, gas and renewable energy. Depending on what I read, my mood swings between optimism and fatalistic pessimism. In the end, though, I am optimistic, putting my faith in the momentum of technology and the self-interest of business to drag the men of yesterday who believe they run Australia into a cleaner, more sustainable future.

Judith Brett

Stephen Bell is professor of political economy at the University of Queensland. His recent co-authored books include *The Rise of the People's Bank of China*, *Masters of the Universe, Slaves of the Market* and *Fair Share: Competing Claims and Australia's Economic Future*.

Judith Brett is emeritus professor of politics at La Trobe University. She won the National Biography Award in 2018 for *The Enigmatic Mr Deakin*. Her other books include *From Secret Ballot to Democracy Sausage*, *Robert Menzies' Forgotten People* and *Australian Liberals and the Moral Middle Class*. She is the author of four Quarterly Essays.

Tim Buckley is the Director of Energy Finance Studies, Australasia, at the Institute for Energy Economics and Financial Analysis.

Peter Christoff is the author, with Robyn Eckersley, of *Globalization and the Environment*, and editor of *Four Degrees of Warming: Australia in a Hot World*. He teaches climate policy at the University of Melbourne.

Andy Lloyd worked for Rio Tinto for twenty-three years, mostly in coal and uranium mining. He was Rio Tinto's representative on the board of the World Coal Institute from 2000 to 2006, and on the Australian Coal Association from 2004 to 2007. He is a past chair of IEA Environmental Projects, the implementing agent for the IEA Clean Coal Centre, and a past chair of the Energy Policy Institute of Australia.

Russell Marks is a lawyer and an honorary research associate at La Trobe University. He is the author of *Crime and Punishment: Offenders and Victims in a Broken Justice System*.

Katharine Murphy has worked in Canberra's parliamentary press gallery since 1996 for the *Australian Financial Review*, *The Australian* and *The Age*, before joining *Guardian Australia*, where she is political editor. She won the Paul Lyneham Award for Excellence in Press Gallery Journalism in 2008 and has been a Walkley Award finalist twice. She was awarded an honorary doctorate by the University of Canberra in 2019. She is a director of the National Press Club and the author of *On Disruption*.

Anna Rose is a climate campaigner and the author of *Madlands: A Journey to Change the Mind of a Climate Sceptic*.

Zoe Whitton leads Citi's Environmental, Social and Governance Research team in Asia, advising institutional investors globally on issues such as climate change and the energy transition.

Coming Soon

Quarterly Essay 80
On Australia and New Zealand
Laura Tingle

Australia and New Zealand are often considered close cousins. But why, despite being so close, do we know so little about each other? And is there such a thing as national character?

In this wise and illuminating essay, Laura Tingle looks at leadership, economics, history and more. Competitiveness has marked our relationship from its earliest days. In the past half-century, both countries have remade themselves amid shifting economic fortunes. New Zealand has been held up as a model for everything from tax reform to the conduct of politics to the response to COVID-19. Tingle considers everything from Morrison and Ardern as national leaders to the different ways each country has dealt with its colonial legacy. What could Australia learn from New Zealand? And New Zealand from Australia?

This is a perceptive, often amusing introduction to two countries alike in some ways, but quite different in others.

Out December 2020

Subscribe so you never miss an issue at **quarterlyessay.com.au/subscribe**

QUARTERLY ESSAY BACK ISSUES

BACK ISSUES: (Prices include GST, postage and handling within Australia.) *Grey indicates out of stock.*

- ☐ **QE 1** ($15.99) Robert Manne *In Denial*
- ☐ **QE 2** ($15.99) John Birmingham *Appeasing Jakarta*
- ☐ **QE 3** ($15.99) Guy Rundle *The Opportunist*
- ☐ **QE 4** ($15.99) Don Watson *Rabbit Syndrome*
- ☐ **QE 5** ($15.99) Mungo MacCallum *Girt By Sea*
- ☐ **QE 6** ($15.99) John Button *Beyond Belief*
- ☐ **QE 7** ($15.99) John Martinkus *Paradise Betrayed*
- ☐ **QE 8** ($15.99) Amanda Lohrey *Groundswell*
- ☐ **QE 9** ($15.99) Tim Flannery *Beautiful Lies*
- ☐ **QE 10** ($15.99) Gideon Haigh *Bad Company*
- ☐ **QE 11** ($15.99) Germaine Greer *Whitefella Jump Up*
- ☐ **QE 12** ($15.99) David Malouf *Made in England*
- ☐ **QE 13** ($15.99) Robert Manne with David Corlett *Sending Them Home*
- ☐ **QE 14** ($15.99) Paul McGeough *Mission Impossible*
- ☐ **QE 15** ($15.99) Margaret Simons *Latham's World*
- ☐ **QE 16** ($15.99) Raimond Gaita *Breach of Trust*
- ☐ **QE 17** ($15.99) John Hirst *'Kangaroo Court'*
- ☐ **QE 18** ($15.99) Gail Bell *The Worried Well*
- ☐ **QE 19** ($15.99) Judith Brett *Relaxed & Comfortable*
- ☐ **QE 20** ($15.99) John Birmingham *A Time for War*
- ☐ **QE 21** ($15.99) Clive Hamilton *What's Left?*
- ☐ **QE 22** ($15.99) Amanda Lohrey *Voting for Jesus*
- ☐ **QE 23** ($15.99) Inga Clendinnen *The History Question*
- ☐ **QE 24** ($15.99) Robyn Davidson *No Fixed Address*
- ☐ **QE 25** ($15.99) Peter Hartcher *Bipolar Nation*
- ☐ **QE 26** ($15.99) David Marr *His Master's Voice*
- ☐ **QE 27** ($15.99) Ian Lowe *Reaction Time*
- ☐ **QE 28** ($15.99) Judith Brett *Exit Right*
- ☐ **QE 29** ($15.99) Anne Manne *Love & Money*
- ☐ **QE 30** ($15.99) Paul Toohey *Last Drinks*
- ☐ **QE 31** ($15.99) Tim Flannery *Now or Never*
- ☐ **QE 32** ($15.99) Kate Jennings *American Revolution*
- ☐ **QE 33** ($15.99) Guy Pearse *Quarry Vision*
- ☐ **QE 34** ($15.99) Annabel Crabb *Stop at Nothing*
- ☐ **QE 35** ($15.99) Noel Pearson *Radical Hope*
- ☐ **QE 36** ($15.99) Mungo MacCallum *Australian Story*
- ☐ **QE 37** ($15.99) Waleed Aly *What's Right?*
- ☐ **QE 38** ($15.99) David Marr *Power Trip*
- ☐ **QE 39** ($15.99) Hugh White *Power Shift*
- ☐ **QE 40** ($15.99) George Megalogenis *Trivial Pursuit*
- ☐ **QE 41** ($15.99) David Malouf *The Happy Life*
- ☐ **QE 42** ($15.99) Judith Brett *Fair Share*
- ☐ **QE 43** ($15.99) Robert Manne *Bad News*
- ☐ **QE 44** ($15.99) Andrew Charlton *Man-Made World*
- ☐ **QE 45** ($15.99) Anna Krien *Us and Them*
- ☐ **QE 46** ($15.99) Laura Tingle *Great Expectations*
- ☐ **QE 47** ($15.99) David Marr *Political Animal*
- ☐ **QE 48** ($15.99) Tim Flannery *After the Future*
- ☐ **QE 49** ($15.99) Mark Latham *Not Dead Yet*
- ☐ **QE 50** ($15.99) Anna Goldsworthy *Unfinished Business*
- ☐ **QE 51** ($15.99) David Marr *The Prince*
- ☐ **QE 52** ($15.99) Linda Jaivin *Found in Translation*
- ☐ **QE 53** ($15.99) Paul Toohey *That Sinking Feeling*
- ☐ **QE 54** ($15.99) Andrew Charlton *Dragon's Tail*
- ☐ **QE 55** ($15.99) Noel Pearson *A Rightful Place*
- ☐ **QE 56** ($15.99) Guy Rundle *Clivosaurus*
- ☐ **QE 57** ($15.99) Karen Hitchcock *Dear Life*
- ☐ **QE 58** ($15.99) David Kilcullen *Blood Year*
- ☐ **QE 59** ($15.99) David Marr *Faction Man*
- ☐ **QE 60** ($15.99) Laura Tingle *Political Amnesia*
- ☐ **QE 61** ($15.99) George Megalogenis *Balancing Act*
- ☐ **QE 62** ($15.99) James Brown *Firing Line*
- ☐ **QE 63** ($15.99) Don Watson *Enemy Within*
- ☐ **QE 64** ($15.99) Stan Grant *The Australian Dream*
- ☐ **QE 65** ($15.99) David Marr *The White Queen*
- ☐ **QE 66** ($15.99) Anna Krien *The Long Goodbye*
- ☐ **QE 67** ($15.99) Benjamin Law *Moral Panic 101*
- ☐ **QE 68** ($15.99) Hugh White *Without America*
- ☐ **QE 69** ($15.99) Mark McKenna *Moment of Truth*
- ☐ **QE 70** ($15.99) Richard Denniss *Dead Right*
- ☐ **QE 71** ($15.99) Laura Tingle *Follow the Leader*
- ☐ **QE 72** ($15.99) Sebastian Smee *Net Loss*
- ☐ **QE 73** ($15.99) Rebecca Huntley *Australia Fair*
- ☐ **QE 74** ($15.99) Erik Jensen *The Prosperity Gospel*
- ☐ **QE 75** ($15.99) Annabel Crabb *Men at Work*
- ☐ **QE 76** ($22.99) Peter Hartcher *Red Flag*
- ☐ **QE 77** ($22.99) Margaret Simons *Cry Me a River*
- ☐ **QE 78** ($22.99) Judith Brett *The Coal Curse*

Please include this form with delivery and payment details overleaf.
Back issues also available as eBooks at **quarterlyessay.com**